# Language Arts Unit

## A RAP TEXTBOOK

# Language Arts Unit

**A RAP TEXTBOOK**

*By Rhys Langston Podell*

# BLK MARKET POETRY

**Black Market Poetry**

1 Langstónia Ln

The Estate, Langstónia 1.01

Langstonia.org

**ISBN** 978-0-578-22962-1

**for**

*my Podell-Recasner-de Marco-Kim family,*
*who have always allowed me to freely create and speak*

**and**

*whatever is the opposite of "for the 'gram"*

# Contents

.

# Foreword (From Here)

*content warning:*
*this collection of words might induce*
*sudden compulsions to roll one's eyes, turn*
*to a thesaurus, revive an academic career,*
*or take any ideas as more than an*
*approximation or suggestion*

### i.

This effort is a rap album as much as a book of poems. It is as much a book of poems as a text/book of faithfully transcribed musical numbers that take you proverbial n[]gg[]s to school. Moreover, the work presents a poet-essayist's album prefaced with a rapper's essay, with both forms to be several questions in the form of several answers— or perhaps answers in the form of questions. It is to marry the erudite and the cool, an insurgency of unconventional meaning through what hopes to be infectious sound.

In prose and in verse-in-song, these two halves present a gift of style and delivery in the form of a *Language Arts Unit:* a unit to measure a self-declared mastery in the elongated and mouthy prose of a rapper unconfined by 16 bar increments, and 11 songs by a calculated writer blurring sound and meaning at will. The intention simply put: to freak the form and the content past any symbiotic expectations; to have the words breathe through the page and bang in any speakers.

Previous musical projects have concerned themselves with form versus content and a literary level of lyrical depth. *Full Frontal Incumbent, An Incongruous Mixtape* teetered between emotional openness and self-effacing abstraction. *Aggressively Ethnically Ambiguous* toyed with the performances and embodiments of race as form and content. *Language Arts Unit,* through its individual song topics, picks up where the latter just began to suggest a firmer savvy and wider scope. A few examples: a nostalgia for early childhood friendship filtered through the jargon of video games through decades; an exposé and case for this writer/orator as the Spotify-friendly poet laureate of his living room; a conversation between generations of a family through decades on many sides of the color line; a sung simile of state-condoned domestic terrorism as a marriage foreshadowing acrimonious divorce proceedings; and so on.

However, unlike the preceding projects (and past absurdist self-anthropologizing or auto-ethnography/biography), these words and music present two forms talking between themselves as a product and response to the context of their creation: in one aspect, to write a lyric essay with sentences as *bars*, proposing a new, verbose sense of *realness* in a take-no-prisoners rapper's ethos of shit-talking between paragraphs; from another angle, to craft a rap album of nuance and expressionist poetics, proposing the form as an essential means of delivering ideas, one able to communicate complexities on various levels of understanding and comprehension.

Though no art is spared consideration of its context, this fusion of disciplines in particular speaks to a fundamental contradiction of its time. That is, one can see a warranted alarmism to be stirred up with under-addressed, existential questions that seem to be increasingly pressing (climate change, systemic, systematic global inequality, unending armed conflict, etc.). Conversely, there is also a new need to reclaim a patience in parsing through information; to find new thresholds of critical thinking when obvious fact is contentiously debated and undermined, and a paradigm of immediacy tethers us with technological rectangles in our pockets. Art across disciplines and media is responding to (or feeling the effect of) such changes and questions, whether critically, unconsciously, or somewhere in between. *Language Arts Unit* represents a hopeful possibility of responding critically and creatively, with a mind to immediacy and the superficial, so as to suggest what is transformatively original may lie in a future of subversions through combinations, re-workings, and a clever coaxing of extended thinking.

Still, if we speak of a future as reflective of where we are today, it does not look all too clear or certain in direction. Many a postmodernist has resisted grand explanations, causalities, or teleologies for *where we are*. Any "universal" theories on language and culture will have us constructing arguments until the end of time (and debating time itself). Even so, from Neolithic gibberish to the slang of yesteryear, memeface to Blackspeech, in dialect, image caption, and in print block, undoubtedly the language arts have served as our translations and tributes. They are stone tablets and speaker phones and phablets. They are as much manner as law, as much clarity as code, passed along through gradients of culture and time. Literature can reflect the state of these arts (however historically emphasizing well-to-do white men), and only after, in perhaps hifalutin theories and historical narratives, are we able to piece together worded language's larger changes. Yet, putting aside that respectful, deconstructionist hat, the work that follows in this album preface risks the possibility of stylistic sleights of hand and elisions in making its confident, rapper-like assertions.

So now allow me to talk my mess with this rap literature, even if I come in close proximity to my discipline's most feared designation: being corny.

## ii.

For an overthinker such as myself, writing and rapping in English, American English, two decades into the 21st century comes with acknowledging that my expression in the language affords me a greater consideration and reach. As much a lingua franca as an ever more hegemonic terms and conditions of sorts, English is the language everyone wants to speak, if they don't already in some form. A global Internet has enabled this primacy past foundations in more blatant (cultural) imperialism.[1] In the current moment (which might be more clearly theorized with a few decades' hindsight), I would argue there are novel changes to its form, content, and scope as these words and etymologies undergo immediate feedback and archiving by handheld computerized, internet technology— that *thing* upon which we have seemingly bet our entire planet's structure and model of progress.

We are deep into a restructuring, with life moving towards completely software-mediated "solutions" and "optimization", and an anxiety that our social contract has become a user end license agreement never quite fully presented to us before the beginning of this process. It's no secret— the concentration of power and geopolitical influence rests in digital networks. It's similarly an open secret that algorithms and other tools of machine learning reflect human error and cultural bias. The admirable computer scientist, musician, and rare white person with dreadlocks that is partly excused, Jaron Lanier, has written, "moral hazard has never met a more efficient amplifier than a digital network" (Lanier 54).[2] For those of us speaking from (and to a lesser extent *for*) positions of the underrepresented, the oppressed, the *less than heard,* or even the young and impatient, this technological dressing can be read as *the same old shit,* now just surrounding us in an omnipotent *cloud.* With the mass of many a writing and rewriting of our human history, progress narratives, and precedents before us and across our screens, to be *woke* is to flirt with being overwhelmed:

We know the unquestioned common tongue of both historical and future space age science fiction as English, where antiquity and our post-Earth futurism are in some form an Americanization of the Queen's English.

Trap music is a vacation weekend in the California desert with VIP passes and a privatized gross domestic production numbering far greater than the amount of feathers found in the legion of college sophomores' "Indian" headdresses. Black is a pre-existing condition for whom its bearers hold the burden of representing both extractable cool and the boogeymen of society; in life, a continuous studio session of audio cash crops, and in death, an immensely retweetable cautionary tale. The syntactical fragmentation found in memes and internet speak is everywhere from Star Wars reboots to the tweet deck of the oval office, the latter whose fraudulent executives run state-sanctioned Twitter farms to hold federal wages hostage and self-incriminate. Nazis have rebranded and are public-relations-friendly, explicit in F.C.C. approved synonyms, while Slovenian Eva Braun pleads the Fifth on all matters, from Obama-era immigrant concentration camps to presidential sexual misconduct. There are more talk shows than ever, writer's rooms brimming with comedians scrambling to re-contextualize everything and define both the trauma and the time it might take to derive a joke from said trauma. Billionaire newsprint sponsored by multinationals' subsidiary companies run equal parts post-irony and post-blasé native advertising. Cabinet-friendly economists and lobbyists continue to argue against transitioning from fossil fuels and the tenability of switching to renewable energy, belying their discipline's assumption of scarcity. The Department of Defense and cloud-based retailers are finding ways to automate out boots on the ground, as one Amazon expands and the other contracts—[3]

*excuse me one moment while I close the twenty tabs in my web browser before this becomes a bizarrely pedantic "listicle" that could go on forever (OMG LOL, I feel seen)—*

On the user end, and from the perspective of someone mildly well-read and healthily skeptical (OK, a disgruntled millennial), the Internet and all its gadgetry presents a determination of reality and perception of time that seems at once absolute, while also immediately subject to change and mood swing. Even the minimal amount of research or usage of these platforms shows evidence that the algorithms and backend source codes increasingly work in such a way that our inputs (selfies, virtue signaling commentaries, post shares, etc.) reflect what is output (tailor-made advertisements, content atop one's feed, push notifications, etc.)— and then input back again (and so forth).* Much what is pinged back in this feedback loop is often what seems the most sensationalist, offensive, or, more aptly, that which is most suited to a consistent news cycle and feed built on dollars-per-click.[4]

My mother— I mean my editor— told me to never write what I couldn't fully defend, but fuck it. The Internet and its encumbered technology/architecture present humanity remixed and reworked, as prone to advanced primate ingenuity as reptilian brain stereotypes. Any expression or art form must encounter this filter and distributor of sorts, if it seeks to present itself as real and to legitimate its existence across the reality of others. It is fooling oneself to say that this isn't a frightening contemplation and creative's given conditions (especially when one's art form is the most prone to simplification in one-dimensional portraiture and immediacy in a love affair with trends).

---

* Corporate advertising money structures the Internet's present model. Algorithmic corners of social media networks, search engines, and media streaming services aggregate populations' inputs and ever-morphing profile details, to churn back the massive and granular data into worlds, sites, apps, content etc. for consumption, and rinse, repeat. The implicit consent to constant surveillance, data collection, and its sale to corporate advertisers as it were, is current the price of "free" internet technologies. Though "big data, like any data, does not represent an objective truth", one would be fooled into believing so, with its use as a "marketing term and a techno-utopian vision" (Lewis and Westlund 7, 3). This model exerts a stranglehold over any other conception of how the Internet could work and thus self-perpetuates.[5]

### iii.

On a timeline such as this, rap and hip-hop music, particularly popular rap (arguably the most powerful manifestation of artfully remixing and reconstituting existing culture into content), has reached pop music's ultimate sanitized and mainstay position. Graduated from a once strictly stereotyped and racially coded young person's symbol of defiance, it is presently worldwide and ubiquitously banal in spectacles with deep pocket production budgets. It is here to stay, and doubly trite are claims that rap is not real music or— *hand flourish*— that it is a literary poetic movement Sir William Shakespeare himself would praise. As the most popular form of music consumed in the U.S., one could similarly make a global case for that position, by virtue of the genres which have appropriated its style and production techniques. As Kevin Young writes of America's long history of plagiarized authorship and imposture, the "Blackfaced person always occupies a bigger stage than a Black one" (Young 389).[1] Indeed, rap's modern ascendance can be described as a foregone conclusion of the emergence of post-racial (read: nonBlack) n[]gg[] *shit and glitz.*

The climes of popular art and music have never been meritocratic, but rap has always fronted the existence of such a system of valuation— you know, *real shit over the wack.* Public relations have long left the corner block, and the corner block has become the smartphone, with spoken rhymers (increasingly crooning) jockeying to self-publish under the pretense of instantaneous feedback, success, and narrowly historical top placement in the swell of the form's popularity. Whereas say, five years ago a successful album or even single drop could earn a rapper six months to a year of renown and publicity, now a release is considered past prime circulation in two months.[2] To make a rap album with the pretense of a public unveiling is to stare into this potential PR nihilism.[*]

A seemingly cottage-industry act of *being-on-the-come-up* has thus advanced from a marginalized form of the American *pulling-oneself-up-by-the-*

---

[*] In fact, as I've written this over a period of close to two years, I've noticed the life cycles get even shorter, to the point where (at least for music conspicuously trying to be "popular") a lack of attention the first few weeks is just short of a death sentence.

*bootstraps* capitalist mythology to full force in this nation's most authentic art form: corporate-backed advertising. We believe that a self-publishing pop culture is such, and not many selves publishing one manicured self or ideal— whether by means of management companies/label arrangements, or independent trend snipers riding waves, making post after post until headway into *the business* is achieved. Posting about "making moves" might indeed be more important than making said moves. One could scroll through a social media newsfeed to see that "the reality of time has been replaced by publicity of time" (Debord 50).[3]

In one vision of the future, on an endless live stream broadcast, everyone might speak in auto-tune, name dropping products they have recently bought, with instant recall to re-record the entirety of every single moment for broadcast on-demand. A&Rs would in turn hustle to interpret a discrete function of metrics to spell how many folks will tune in before they tune in, who will exist before they exist, and what trends might be predicted, negating any need for further socialized engineering. Of course, the last forecast is laughable, as it is a tired joke the plethora of popular culture phrases, trends, and phenomena that have been mined from those who make "underground" art or those whose very persons have been societally demarcated "underground" (see "on fleek" and its corporate monetization without compensation, "classic rock 'n' roll" and white fathers with stunted music taste, trans women of color at Stonewall and masculinist whitewashing of "Pride," etc.).[4]

**iv.**

This is all to say immediacy is, if not *the* essence, at least a fundamental quality of today, trappings and all. A trap rap song can be made well, very fast, finalized, and intravenously put into *the culture* same day. The "Rap Caviar" Spotify playlist, consequently more resembles "Rap McDonald's", and Genius verified video breakdowns, well, dumb shit. Though proclaimed dead many times in the womb, the backslash fraternal twins of hip-hop/rap have continued a half-stepping maturity through the Internet, about as disinterestedly desensitized as any other young person with access to instantly available vaults of reality "television," violent video games, and hardcore pornography.

The underground, in the overwhelming reality of a rap renaissance in all sub-genres, has been proclaimed *over*, and major labels find themselves reversing their tactics of yore, looking for what is viral and profitable before putting forward an offer or cent of a cash advance. What is "profitable and viral," is increasingly everything but the music itself: participation in a clone war of three letter name prefixes, an ability to reference apropos and in vogue pharmaceutical drugs, an inflammatory and trending web presence, a standardization of regional slang, clothing, hair style/color, etc. This positive feedback loop of corporate crowdsourcing (if we are to believe there aren't hands in the pot before formal deal announcements) now sees bigger dividends in rap than ever before. Like the cold snaps and heat waves across the changing climate of the world, Billboard charts are breaking records for how many records are being broken, not fully reckoning with the idea that the records for the record industry we have constituted thus far indicate a free-market-based myopia in how a musical and pop cultural lineage is conceived.[1]

Though of course depending if one asks Guy Debord, Francis Fukuyama, or Sun Ra, history either ended or began to end in the 1950s, after taking two sabbaticals following 1776 and somewhere near the end of the Roman Empire. Now in our 21st century modernity, measured by over twenty iPhone models, a Blackface Black Jew is only crucified on a rap diss and midtown Manhattan Nero only watches his cabinet burn, leaving further arson to those who have stuck around. It is possible both are on a front page, somewhere/everywhere in a news cycle akin to a 24/7 three-fifths compromise in a golden age of controversy and outrage, where a majority who lost the popular vote believes its demands are the only ones worthy of consideration because it is both silent and loud enough. Indeed those who use words with the most gusto paradoxically are those who obviously do not read, widely or at all, and might just proudly proclaim that.[2]

But in all seriousness, our present moment can feel as though from a single point and everywhere at once (like a YouTube unboxing video of an uncased universe) our supposedly consensus culture and the very perception of what exists is instantaneously flooding out from the multimedia contained on the Internet and enabled by computer technologies. At an intersection like this, such a bombardment often disallows for a full stop and consideration to inspect of the volume of legitimate oncoming hazards. Among innumerable challenges posed by this climate of the immediate, is a growing sense of euphemism, misdirection, and well, bullshit only enabled by the rapidity of information and difficulty in parsing it before the next time a refresh button is pressed.

Rap might seem a low stakes operation in contrast to such a flurried landscape, but as a totalizing force of pop culture and a continually powerful fusion of stereotype and reclaiming of agency, it feeds into and feeds the ecosystem of information with which we are presented. Rap is fully integrated into the corporate mesh which encases and takes precedent in all matters of this modern world. It is a thoroughly modern and fascinating contradiction of both entrenched ideology and an artful response to it.

We must now consider that like and unlike other moments in time, our collective language and means of expression are being reshaped and appropriated by unprecedented means of technology, and particularly that as Black orators there is a new dimension to our tongues' weight. Our subversions and reworking of phrases have been so removed from our cultural context (however that boundary can be drawn) that those who now use them believe what is literally said, whether in a court or law* or in an automated newsfeed, human or machine. *Bad* really meaning *good* seems to have been confused for a way to make a malleable morality of rights and wrongs, like an Orwellian bureaucrat after spending a few months as a sleeper cell in the Black Panther party, on the up and up, thinking he's really *down*, perhaps even forgetting he flipped *good* to *bad* just to add proverbial swag. No wonder a Russian bot is as American as it gets.

---

* I look to the recent cases (and some resulting convictions) wherein lyrics have been used to indict rappers for murder and other crimes. Of course, that is not assuming that violent expressions in art are rather, in a true colorblind interpretation, quintessential American culture.[3]

**v.**

With word-first music (by far and away the most currently popular), the lyrics and music both appeal and attract. Having American English as a shield bearer of universally cool cultural imperialism, the famous quartet of pop rap lyricism— *fuck, bitch, n[]gg[], shit* — might then be as catchy as a specific melodic arrangement. Like other musical motifs, specifically those in pop music, through constant immersion these become necessary to the point of addiction— to the point where we do not hear or very consciously experience them anymore. Nonetheless, somewhere along the line we expect the appearance of one of these four words, as much we anticipate a hard snare and kick sample, or a high level of compression on the whole song.

We surely have reached a peak in this disco era of trap music to where, if mixed right, anything can sound *perfect* and *sweet* to the ears, from a point of mastery of this form's balancing act of production. It is worth wondering if a song would be as catchy and seductive to the senses if it had the same beat, melody, and/or flow pattern with simply different words and concepts used than what is expected. Or is there something essential about the baseline pool of ideas and words that has been established? Does the rate and immediacy with which songs are made disallow references to synonyms, or re-examinations of the whole picture and message given by compositions?

There are plenty examples of further questions to ask: is a song about serving narcotics, doing pharmaceutic drugs, and shooting all that blissful or relaxing when we turn it on in a party setting, or have we become ok with some normative levels of anxiety, perhaps even a meta-commentary to suggest that, with social ills so far gone, anxiety is what is most calming to us? Would it be useful to apply the Bechdel test or a better yet a *Suga Free test* in evaluating if the still male-centric medium can go a full album without referencing a "bitch" (one who is a man's protectorate, largely a demonstration of his property and exertion of power)? Is it mansplaining to suggest some female rappers have appropriated toxic masculinity? Further, might we scrutinize the "androgynous misogynists" in our midst, who stand in for superficial progressions of masculine identity, without much lyrical content substantive enough to call for departures from how gender and sexuality are constructed along lines of exclusion and subjugation?[1]

Still, If the pejorative *mumble rap* is supposed to suggest a degradation of language, we must also consider another view. Might post-lyrical, post-conscious rap be the shuffling off of the yoke of English, a language forcefully grafted onto a people whose innovations and re-workings go perpetually under-recognized at an institutional level? Such can be seen as an act of ownership and reclamation, wherein there is a retooling oneself against standards of what is deemed respectable, professional, or otherwise slyly implied as "white." However, one must reframe and rethink ideas of ownership when it is on the biggest stage in the world, when that ownership has a licensing deal split four or five ways, when that ownership is owned, is subjected to A&R R&D, made to uphold the incentives of a boardroom, becomes viral with tertiary streaming royalties holding fealty to focus groups who cannot focus past the time it takes two-thirds of an Instagram story to expire.

The metaphorical symbol of "the Elvis" no longer applies when Sprite's advertising arm of confirmation bias has made it the drink of hip-hop aka urban communities aka negroes; when a Black girl ghostwrites for the culturally pioneering white, ghettoized meme-to-trapstar Bhad Bhabie; when the conscious rapper label became a singular name and then meme who interviewed another meme for the church of clicks; and when a phenotypically "nonBlack-looking" Latino artist, appropriating Japanese for his namesake (and on his way to an almost prophetic set of criminal charges and corresponding plea deal after a strong year's run of semi-clandestine corporate backing), dropped *that* word in his songs more than his Black contemporaries.[2]

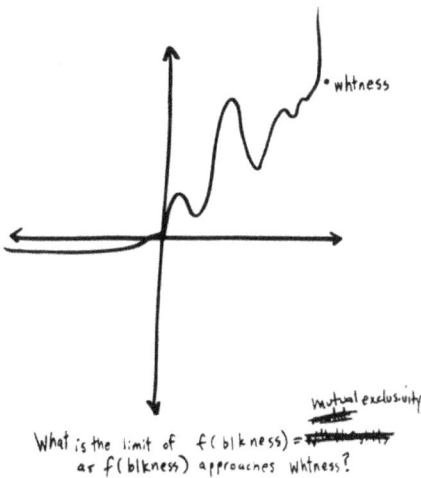

• whtness

mutual exclusivity

What is the limit of  f( blkness) = ~~~~~~~~
as f(blkness) approaches whtness?

Rap is post-appropriation*, and if its marketing is to be believed, so is its associated blackness. However post-appropriated, it still has not been completely gentrified. The question is will it ever be, with a perennial cultural insistence on a hood narrative, one in which Black folk are supposedly pathologically predestined? Is there liberation to be sought in this moment for Black people to possibly gaze beyond a level of authenticity being solely tied to a proximity of criminality, poverty, subjugation, and "carrying the bulk of the load" of being a permanent underclass? Even in a melting pot, non-dichromatic racial reality, "blackness has been associated with a certain sense of decay, even when that decay is invoked in the name of a certain (fetishization of) vitality" (Moten 177).[3]

The multiple personality disorder of hip-hop's appropriation is easily apparent. Record label categories under the slightest scrutiny reflect political discourse, with urban/hip-hop as euphemism for Black and rural/country for white. Both the initial controversy surrounding Lil Nas X's "Old Town Road"'s country-rap ascendance to record-breaking fame and recent electoral cycles' talking points erasing the reality of nonwhite, rural, working class people bring this into sharp relief. There is certainly a ceiling to rap's appropriation and its absorption into a "proper" body politic of culture.† Or as the sighing maxim goes, "everybody wanna be a n[]gg[], but nobody wanna be a n[]gg[]."[4]

---

* Post-appropriation of rap could be theorized as a complicated and subtle intersectional, horizontal appropriation, wherein people at least varying degrees removed from hegemonic power appropriate hip-hop in more "horizontal" displays" (from 88rising's ascendance alongside Chinese neocolonial presence in Africa and the Caribbean, to the powder from Andean people's coca leaf repossessed by middle class rappers as authentically *hood* in "coke raps" mostly consumed in white suburban ears). Or it may be simply the point beyond which the appropriated form can be argued as "rightfully" claimed by its originators. In colloquial terms it would be the argument that "it's everyone's culture as long as you are *hip-hop*" (from white terrorist Richard Spencer obliviously tweeting phrases with roots in ebonics and hip-hop culture, to no eyes blinked at the highest selling hip-hop artist of all time being a white man, even and especially as his recent output sullies the small collection of well done albums which catapulted his fame).[5]

† One can look to the under-acknowledged skin dyeing of Ariana Grande, and the hair and makeup choices by the royal influencer family, the Kardashians, wherein gender and race are in a particular matrix of tangled revisionism. The appropriation is not simply Black girl aesthetics but *light-skinned* Black girl aesthetics. It seems those without a membership to the open secret society of blackness have ran out of things to appropriate and are now going for our particular brand of colorism.[6]

Post-appropriation of rap and its unresolved entanglement of blackness might be a framework in which to think, with hip-hop and rap decades past the point of globalization. American blackness, if nothing else, is inclusive of its mixed membership, but the diaspora around the world delineates blackness differently, in that the American one-drop-rule, while no longer legally binding, reflects a legacy of forced solidarity among people who might have vastly differing experiences. The cliché refrain of "we are not a monolith" is nonetheless important to revisit, as anti-blackness is evolving with the double-sided coin of multiculturalism and the ever-transparent and virulent resistance to it. While anti-Black colorism in American contexts has not quite pervaded a cultural consciousness like it has in Latin American countries (because in the very least conservative white America's perpetual refusal to consider nonwhites authentically, essentially American), it is a mainstay, from the lighter skin shades of marquee, token Black TV and film roles to the multiracial backgrounds of prominent Black political figures.[7]

Rap's co-optation as *everyone's* with its continual insistence on an authentic dark-skinned Black masculine thug trope is a type of gaslighting as efficiently contradictory as it is seemingly deadlocked. While something like Kwame Anthony Appiah's "rooted cosmopolitanism" of shared humanity might eventually be aspired to with the global embrace of this art form, blackness as a politically revolutionary designation and hip-hop as its referent remain unresolved.[*] It's vital to splinter here and say, rap and hip-hop are not the same. Rap is a musical practice and technique birthed from hip-hop, by its nature as technique, able be sprinkled in different musical styles.[†] Hip-hop is of a spirited lineage skirting permission to proceed, a la jazz, the blues, pre-

---

[*] Of course such unresolved contradictions are entirely the point of Appiah's discourse. As he writes, "what I want to make plausible is, instead, a form of universalism that is sensitive to the ways in which historical context shape a practice" (Appiah 256).[8]

[†] I shall reiterate: *rap is a musical practice* (done by musicians!!). An individual with no listening knowledge, simply reading or hearing about rap by proxy would think it some anomaly of performance, as it is most prone to use in parody, totally disregarded by local live talent booking, and even thrown under the bus by the rappers who make it. Of course, this is all indebted to its frequently brusque content and the people who are most associated with the practice. As purportedly post-racial as one would make it out to be, the lack of respect for rap musically still means it is *n[]gg[] shit*. As such, the comments of rappers declaring they are "not rappers" but "musicians" recall the apocryphal "I'm not Black, I'm O.J." quote.[9]

gentrified rock 'n' roll, free breakfast programs, illegal reading by sparse candlelight after enslaved fieldwork, etc. Soliciting corporate sponsorship, creating with mind to an economic bottom line, and surrendering to lyrical conventions is certainly a form of asking for the right to proceed— but even under this sycophancy hip-hop is not dead. It remains ever important to call upon the words of Saidiya Hartman in saying, "a Black revolution makes everyone freer than they actually want to be."[10]

**vi.**

Have we narrowed our possibilities by modeling and shaping our very expressions on refashioning, sampling, or negating what has already existed before and what we only anticipate will exist next? And who is that we, and what inclusion surrounds that us? If we see as a sort of poetic— albeit insufficient— reparations our unique Black American diction and expressionism now spread across the world through popular culture, we have to firmly look at what that signifies. They might not be seen as subversive any longer, which begs the question: if we are continued to be mined atop a corporate-to-consumer pyramid for our authenticity and the coolness of a perceived danger we represent and/or hold at bay, is there the need or possibility to create a new iteration?

To stay relevant, or to simply exist across scrolling timelines, it is supposed that Black artists must either refute or reify existing stories, without a third option of stepping away: into a linguistic boycott, a politics of disengagement, a nicely auto-tuned "no" and nothing more, a sit-in with glossy electronic production and a microphone, etc. This would not be a capitulation or an appealing address to an outside group who consumes our images, but a self-sustaining ecosystem of expressions so packed with unconcerned *realness* or being *with the shits,* that its specificities, absurdities, and peculiar boredoms elude belief to those who do not exist inside it.*

> if not yourself, I suggest you find the nearest Black
> person who might provide you with a story or two
> about being "out-Blacked" by a nonBlack individual.
> or, if you aren't in proximity of one or have any
> Black people's phone numbers, my Black friend can
> help you for a small fee.

------------------------

* This might be what Paul Beatty coins "unmitigated [b]lackness" in his 2015 novel *The Sellout,* or "the power of not giving a fuck," and more abstractly, "essays passing for fiction" (Beatty 277).[1] However, his book too ends on a note of complicating what is ours and what isn't, and the impossibility of determining such a thing.

This may be as extreme as letting white and nonBlack people have "n[]gg[]," if they desire so much to describe themselves as such. With the edginess finally exhausted, people could finally fulfill their desire to be a n[]gg[] whenever they see fit: pumped up on the treadmill blasting Top 40 music, hands folded at the corporate luncheon, DMing rap videos to classmates during lectures on cultural appropriation, even with the help of a cue card on daytime television. Perhaps, with such a word, they would cease to compare it to us and see in it only themselves, and the fleeting notion they have of *n[]gg[]dom*; that they want their cake and to guillotine it too. This will be when the words do not match their respective language (language being everything but the words, an unfiltered language being the body, the body being the first lexicon and place in a continuum of meaning).*

This is how race is both form and content. To try and make post-race-race-music is as much a tussle through a thought experiment as trying to argue against the concept of race while emphasizing its social and structural realities. One cannot speak as a "real" Black person unless one embodies that weight of history, a history acknowledged or not. As one speaks, the body, standing or sitting in for history, itself modulates the room or space it occupies, changing the possible content of anything mentioned after.[2]

> *in case you don't understand, my Black friend here will explain it to you on behalf of all of us, as a part of a free trial offer:*
>
> - *blackness is at once outwardly self-referential and in conversation with no one.*

---

* Even as I flirt with racial essentialism here, Manuel Arturo Abreu writes far more seriously and comprehensively of this in his *Online Imagined Black English*: "Many times these cross-racial language behaviors do not correspond to most African Americans' linguistic patterns....The Internet allows for communication and media dissemination to a wider and more diffuse audience than was once possible: individuals and communities with less and less relationship to Black media and linguistic behavior have access to it, with Urban Dictionary and Genius (formerly Rap Genius) only a few clicks away to provide 'definitions'" (Abreu, "Online Imaged Black English"). Similarly, Kevin Young writes of "ventriloquism on a high scale, one in which Black folks are commonly used to express 'the truth' or realness without thought of the consequences on them as actual people" (Young 128).[3]

- *It is an inside joke you don't learn but know firsthand.*
- *You can accessorize it with affectations but it can be most true naked.*
- *You cannot neither engineer, produce, nor master it.*
- *blackness cannot be explained in bullet points or lyric essays.*
- *It is toe notes after footnotes, caveats after final draft submissions.*
- *blackness, after continuous attempts to be sold, only really bargains with the mercy of what it could otherwise do with the depth of its anger and vengeance.*

It could be argued harnessing a rebellious nature would instead be all the more reason to sing the chorus of pop music expletives and clichés on even higher registers. The suggestion of a complete migration from this status quo is neither practical nor entirely desired (an artistic landscape replete with linguistically over-esoteric hotep rappers and artists is a bad fever dream in itself). Furthermore, I think after nearly half a millennium of the insistence on exceptional negro achievements to get halfway to positions or presuppositions of power, the emergence of a widespread Black mediocrity, in fact, can be seen as slightly progressive.

However, if this alleged middling within coercive boundaries instead continues to speak for the totality of blackness, we must demonstrate the width of our gradient, to remind *ourselves* in a time when a scale of history and time can feel dictated by seven-to-ten second video loops and algorithmic newsfeeds. This could be a consideration, even a simple thought, toward mixing it up, especially by those who are established with firm foundations of cultural currency. In more ways than the production, going off the rails and beyond the track to create a new default, or at least imagine the possibility. I think there are many who are doing this consciously and subconsciously, though I find spelling it out to reaffirm it critical, so that what we collectively define as alternative is not still somewhat conservative.*

    If this is the default, we must ask what it means that we are circling in these means of expression and baseline content; what it means to desire this, and to be desired to remain so— and if that shackled futurism too is a trap.† Or, in the words of the great Saul Williams, that "your current frequencies of understanding outweigh that which has been given for you to understand."4

---

* When pondering these questions, I consistently think back to an episode in season two of the surrealist network TV show *Atlanta*. Near the beginning of the episode, one of the main characters, Darius, is attempting to pick up a free piano at the estate of a reclusive musician. A conversation briefly brings up the common cleave between generations of Black music taste after he's offered the guest food and drink. "What is it with hip-hop? It seems to have never left its adolescent stage," asks Donald Glover as Teddy Perkins, a stark stand-in and caricature of the King of Pop post-vitiligo-and-nose-reduction. Darius quickly responds, "Sometimes, you know, people just wanna have a good time." And as much as I want to agree with Lakeith Stanfield's soft assurance as Darius in that line, I would like to think the strength of his acting is to communicate that it is what his character might think in the moment, in the way that sometimes a lazy response is best, so as to deflect an uncomfortable or tiresome conversation. The question is not if one is allowed to have a good time expressing one's self as one wishes. The question is, do those who enjoy the *good* time of the music enjoy it for more and longer than the people from whom it was sourced? And further, why is hip-hop only ever painted with one brushstroke, disallowed the complexity of mood and style afforded other genres of music?5

† Simone White echoes this in her *Dear Angel of Death,* saying, "it is a trap in the same sense that trap music proposes as authentic Black life the deadly workaday circuit of street-level drug dealing to pay the bills and, with luck, hard work and a ride-or-die trap queen, bootstrap up to the (clownish) status of a rich n[]gg[]" (White 149). Her work is in conversation with storied analyses of Fred Moten and Saidiya Hartman. Moten's *In the Break* makes the claim for the breadth of Black expression and Black life as a continual improvisation, and contemporary (t)rap certainly suggests a coercion of blackness into a series of boundaries, limits, and predictable scripts. Hartman's theory of "Burdened Individuality of Freedom" complicates the notion of freedom before and after emancipation, in describing the idea of "nascent individualism" following emancipation in its "double bind of freedom: being freed from slavery and free of resources, emancipated and subordinated, self-possessed and indebted, equal and inferior, liberated and encumbered, sovereign and dominated, citizen and subject" (Hartman 35, 36). The overwhelming evidence of corporate control of media and Black creative labor (from movie studios to major record labels to even the presses which publish Black thought and criticism), articulate a certain intractable binding to sounds, images, and ideas successfully presented as solely Black folks' own doing and perpetuating.6

**vii.**

As a rapper, pretenses of *realness* denote the vast catalogue of preconceived notions and stereotypes implicating race, class, and gender detailed ad nauseam in my preceding words. A rapper by trade, my currency is *realness*. However, I take *realness* as recognizing, in my own sphere, the distinct things I can't front. As one might have inferred, I am an unreliable narrator who speaks and writes in terms that I compulsively designate and re-designate as unpossessed (whether in pseudo-academic prose or musical recordings). These terms provide a frequent mirror in knowing I'm so light-complected and facially ambiguous those who vehemently disagree with me might try to void my claim to blackness to invalidate my words. (No indulgences in tragic mulatto lamentations, and not the exhausted aside that I am *too anything* for *any side*.) Rather I am made to be reminded I *am* or am *on* the color line, the *can* in "can pass." (I am the second son of two adjacent relayers in an oppression olympics. My (ad)mix(ture) is a great punchline or a point of analysis in postcolonial, comparative race research: eastern European Jews fleeing pogroms land at Ellis Island adjoin Louisiana sharecropping descendants of those enslaved and raped for free labor. Both ends it should be noted converged at a comedy club.) In a post-appropriation world, where blackness has been made makeup and aesthetic, simultaneously thieved as everyone's and policed as authentic in its fetishized exclusion, I find my axiom of that identity in the non-essentialist, the strange, and the disruptive. In this, I acknowledge my politics of disengagement is different from fellow rappers in my access to different language and musical taste, an insurgent proximity to whiteness, and radically conciliatory skepticism. And so here I am, leaning into the clear parody that is writing thousands of words on manufactured fixation, attention (spans), and reclaiming what a sense of immediacy can be.

Generally speaking, *realness* and truth are intertwined but the latter does not always guarantee the former.* Namely, in a nation of two party politics (which holds the most global influence and military power), admissions of oversight, folly, or even attributions of credit where it is due— like a presidential blow job or reparations for slavery— are as much political suicide as cultural faux pas. Unflinching hubris is the paradigm of *realness* today, only enabled by the occasional disingenuous public apology and paid administrative leave. There has never been more incentive to front.† After a few drinks even a prototypical centrist reformist will admit this stalemate doesn't really lend itself to progress forward.[1] Not to be mistaken with acknowledging "both sides" and blindly, falsely equating matters like fascism and anti-fascism, new foundations of *realness* are in order, beyond our current conceptions. This new sensibility must embody a rejuvenated, no, wholly remade sense of accountability and self-reflection— that is, if we want to be honest about the inert, proverbial *wheels of change* regarding the most vulnerable in our world (please save your eye rolls and temporarily excuse this 2012 Kendrick Lamar song in paragraph form).

Those in the next centuries, reclining in their automated speedboats whipping around the oceans of Oklahoma and Mongolia, might browse the web archives of our present human civilization and see us now as only

---

* The previously cited *Bunk: The Rise of Hoaxes, Humbug, Plagiarists, Phonies, Post-Facts, and Fake News* by Kevin Young, traces the rise of hoaxes, fake-news, and other popularized untruths from the emergence of the penny press to the American presidential election of 2016. In Young's encyclopedic case he declares truth as "not as an absolute or relative, but a skill—a muscle, like memory", and lies and intentional, extravagant fictions as a product of a cultural tendency to rely on euphemism, stereotypes and "exploiting the schism between 'official' language and the vernacular, the politician and the constituent, the self that commits the crime and the self that seeks to get out of it." As he only briefly writes in his conclusion, nowadays this is empowered by a rapid-fire news cycle which is increasingly reliant on internet information algorithms, a combined phenomenon "both too fast and too slow to engender fact-checking" (Young 447, 435, 442).[2]

† Sasha Baron Cohen's *Who Is America?* took this phenomenon to task, blowing out of proportion several public figures' convictions with his absurdist interviewing techniques and devising of incriminating scenarios. One such figure and public servant was a Georgia State Representative who resigned after seeing the backlash at the litany of offensive words he was "duped" into saying. Yet, Dave Chapelle's "When Keeping It Real Goes Wrong" sketch is still the hallmark of parodying this phenomenon, funny given his ever-present doubling down on somewhat reactionary jokes, and resistance to reframing his sense of accountability or sensitivity.[3]

partially equipped to deal with the threshold of computer technologies' advanced transformative power. Their comparative historical lenses might see that folks got off relatively easily in their contemporary backlash and outrage at "cancel culture," compared to the more violent developments that await us in the coming decades, or those of watershed, historical moments like the Bolshevik and Haitian revolutions.

With humanity expanding toward undeniable dependance on advanced, inextricably linked technology, questions of *realness* are deep in narrowing gulfs between, and ever-false dichotomies of, human and machine, truths and untruths— or even thesis and antithesis if one would want to get Hegelian, with it (sorry, I just have Wikipedia and my days off work). The synthetic, the organic, the synthesis, the constituent parts are swirling. A "fake deep" conspiracy video can be substantiated in *deepfake* videos. Cultural appropriation may find its endgame the imminent life form of humanoid artificial intelligence and seek to complete the summoning seance of digital blackface (now faithfully circulated by devotees in animated gifs, hyper-adaptive text ebonics, and improperly colored emojis).[*] Automation and a coming question of universal basic income might bring sentient factory robots to argue for the existence of their souls in flocks to protestantism and come to a moralizing view of their inexhaustible work ethic.[4] *It is what is* ain't what it used to be.

The opposable thumb, which distinguished primates' evolutionary capacity from many animals, continues to facilitate our development as a species, though one would question the form of evolution, this tapping on the soft contact glass of smartphones. Whereas the scroll was once the source of prophecy, now in its continual motion up and down we instead proffer our avatars and effigies, selfies and meme captions, half-baked opinions and pseudo-intellectual analyses into the feed to be spelled out before us again— in the hopes that we might bear the subtle change we hoped for. An elaborate game of telephone it would be (for those playing the pun game at home).

---

[*] One can already see the seeds of this in constructs like Bina48 and Lil Miquela. The former is a Black female robot designed entirely by white men, while the latter (similarly female) is a digital influencer, hand curated by a multi-ethnic staff of millennials, manufactured to be mass marketable as simultaneously ethnically ambiguous and tapped into the aesthetic market of Black affect.[5]

**viii.**

Even if we are resistant to the notion of it, news coverage's use of tweets already foreshadows that Twitter will be one of several primary sources for future chronicling of historical narratives, even and especially in its whole daily flood of unhinged thought under character (assassination) limits. In all its banality, however, the shit-sifting through what is valuable presents questions of immediacy in critical thinking, in addition to a paradoxical patience which we might not be able to afford. Twitter's refusal to introduce an edit button (thankfully) still doesn't address greater powers of revisionism like destructions and burnings of libraries, the "mishandling" of government emails (like those in relation to the war crimes perpetuated during the second Iraq war), or user data being uploaded exclusively on servers the users neither own nor operate. Further and most presently, we have seen the 45th president utilize the brevity and impact of said internet platform to misdirect from the more complex and articulate points of important, concurrent events happening (and under said character limits perhaps intimate nuclear war).[1] Beyond a simple shortsightedness, however, this present firing off of uninhibited opinion as information through algorithms and internet distribution puts us at risk for being extremely presentist— or at least tangled in so much falsity that disentanglement is a project in its own right. Synthesis and synthesizing information might be *the* question of our time.

Advocacy groups and centers of research have proposed refining and exalting the project and doctrine of widespread digital literacy, with what seems an end goal of equipping coding proficient students and children with the means to construct programs and re-interpret or perfect backend measures like algorithms. The intent is to apparently keep oiling the systems in place as if institutional and structural animus will disappear by simply

strange days are these
when I must remind myself
"I am not the Internet"

adding more inclusive actors and agents.* Not that there isn't a CNN-friendly, centrist goal in a Jaron Lanier vision of reclaiming an information economy "toward paid information with a stronger middle class than ever before." Perhaps it is a millennial economic nihilism asserting itself here, but I can't believe that a transformation of the world economy through technology has to be seen as the end-all solution.† Even Lanier himself admits, "we technologists don't usually feel a need to talk about our psychological or cultural ideas," and "the very idea of artificial intelligence gives us the cover to avoid accountability by pretending that machines can take on more and more human responsibility" (Lanier 9, 139, 192).[2]

  With all this talk about time being saved and processes beings streamlined with technology, the question remains: what are we going to do with all the time we will supposedly save? A warranted alarmism shall bring us to wonder how learning, knowledge production, and thinking processes will change. It's doubtful in ordering food to our doorstep, letting cars drive themselves, or having localized security drones patrol our front yards, the bulk of humanity (or those privileged with early access to these developments)[3] is going to "fill" the time by turning to things like abstract

---

* In revealing the gradual transformation of racial subjection in American legal institutions, Michelle Alexander's *The New Jim Crow: Mass Incarceration in the Age of Colorblindess* does much analytical and investigative work in tracing how euphemism and legalese allowed such racial bias and subjugation to reshape itself into a outwardly colorblind paradigm (such that declaring its racial intent seems delusional). It is worth extrapolating (by a more seasoned theorist than *this motherfucker*) the implications for the ways in which computer technologies will enable bureaucrats and techo-salvationists, like euphemism and legalese, to intentionally or unintentionally perpetuate fundamental, structural inequities with this novel distortion of language and masking of intent. There are further questions to ask and theorize. Have digital deliveries allowed for English, increasingly the global language, to not just contain but *become* Newspeak? Will transhumanism provide the biological basis for racism that has been disproven many times over?[4]

† In one indication of how rapid developments are taking place, since the second edition of Lanier's *Who Owns the Future?* five years ago, crypto-currency (with its utopian vision of decentralized money and perfectly ledgered economics) has seen a familiar trend of early adoption and concentration of its holdings in circles of white and Asian men (among some exceptions). As well, major financial institutions have started secretly buying in while demeaning the whole enterprise before the general public in the press. Reports have even suggested crypto-currency's role in facilitating hate groups' extremism, by virtue of the anonymity of its blockchain technology.[5]

theory in bettering our understandings of *everything*.* In my pessimistic optimism, I believe the futures of learning, possibilities of knowledge production, and most centrally, methodologies of socially just resistance will have to emerge in forms and ways that are adaptive to capturing attention and gradual in their coaxing of greater cognitive abilities.

If the content delivery of our phones is any prediction, media and information is moving in modular, bite-sized directions, implying a future of quick attention-getting, acknowledgement of multi-tasking, and emphasis on sequel structure. Though there will always be a space for seemingly purer art forms like hardcover novels, vinyl records, or highway billboard advertising, we seem to forget that such forms evolved from earlier iterations, which became streamlined with incorporation of previously unseen, unheard, or unfelt conventions and configurations. This peak era of television on computers might give us a hint as to how ideas and stories may circulate from this point forth. Though broken into chunks, the prevailing order and cultural mode is to binge these series of visuals when one can, not so much because we cannot pay attention, but that rapt attention must be also able to be divided, paused, and resumed at will.

Now, this essay has shelled out a plethora of mixed metaphors, and two more will serve in this bombardment: those of the iceberg and the rabbit hole. Respectively, one serves to describe certain hidden levels of complexity, while the other conceives of the passage down such levels and details. Internet memes represent a bit of both metaphors in their evolution, with their shift from early 2000s origins in middle school humor to a present emergence as *the* meta-commentary of our time. They demonstrate the tip of an iceberg of accumulated perspectives/experiences, knowledge (or misinformation), inside jokes, and re-contextualized source materials. In creating a meme on the Internet, scrolling through variations, or investigating the origins of the expressed ideas, inevitably one will come away bearing

---

* A.I. education is already being implemented in small provisions. In its guinea pig period it is fair to be cautious, knowing the ways in which standardized education can reflect even the subtlest propaganda and narrowed thinking patterns. Combined with machine learning's tendency to reinforce itself and our human oversights, we must look to new types of agency and adaptability in the face of inevitable structural changes. The athlete and artist philanthropists in our midst cannot solely account for and rectify the contemporary and historical holes in formal educational systems.[6]

*something*. Whether it is a short laugh, an embarrassing moment of agreement, or a fully radicalized ideology, these are small units in systems of information.[*] Informal and formal actors recognize this (like rappers and teachers, or advertising firms and schools) in a much more sanitized, less radical version of say, a Paulo Freire "effort to present significant dimensions of an individual's contextual reality" (Freire 104).[7] Indeed I remember the sharp warmth of my facepalm during my substitute teacher training, when my instructors hammered home didactic points with the most formulaic dad joke memes possible.

Art and media must stare down this elephant that has entered the chatroom (ok, a few more metaphors). For those seeking something more lasting than a momentary top position in an algorithmic news feed, a sensibility of the superficial and the immediate must intersect with a foundation in scalable depth and methods of engagement. One must create this metaphorical iceberg with a captivating enough surface tension to invite a trip down into the unconventional, the surprising, and all ensuing and meticulously devised details.[†] Perhaps I should have pursued a master's degree in marketing to realize what advertisers have known for decades or longer. Or more *on brand*, maybe I should have alienated more readers and argued at an extended length that internet memes effectively showcase a

---

[*] The spread of white nationalist terrorist propaganda through internet memes, image boards, and YouTube recommendation algorithms is certainly evidence of these icebergs and rabbit holes and the dark side of their efficiencies. In fact, the whole ascendancy of contemporary rightwing American politics (to be safe, let's say Obama onwards) has been dependent on calculated misinformation campaigns and clever fragmentation and refashioning of ideas as supposedly revelatory. For (one extreme) example, once one strips away the delivery in internet/satellite radio, web articles, YouTube videos, memes, esoteric subreddit postings, etc., a Glenn Beck, Ben Shapiro, or InfoWars conspiracy about tyrannical world government (as a proxy for fears of liberalism) bears remarkable resemblance to paragraphs of George Wallace's infamous 1963 "Segregation Forever" speech.[8]

[†] Yet, there seems a limit to an appropriation or reclamation of superficiality and preconceived notions. I look to the life and death of Nipsey Hussle, a father, rapper, businessman, philanthropist, Rollin' 60s affiliate, and *real n[]gg[]* (among other roles). He leveraged his gang ties into respect beyond territory and set, self-started musical independence and renown, pioneered entrepreneurial and social justice initiatives, and accrued a general mythos as a constructor of new conceptions Black wealth. On March 31st, 2019, just before he was set to meet with LAPD to discuss mitigating gang violence, he was gunned down in front of the flagship store of his brand and company. Even after LAPDs exaltation of his life's work and public mourning, months later they posthumously continued an investigation into his business for purported gang affiliation and activity.[9]

unique, widespread epistemology in their ability to sustain themselves in the rapidity of algorithms' feedback, in their reduction of complex ideas to peculiarly formatted commentaries, and their consequential usage of elements of immediacy and superficiality. But I am an artist, a rapper, and I instead choose to practice what I overthink.

In all genuine arrogance, what this book and album represent together is a hopeful miscegenation of artistic and critical forms to be competitive to the attention spans and changing thought processes of our time and beyond. One may find a single from this project's audio, based on an interest in its cover art or press photo (yeah, I'm pretty good looking). The beat and instrumental of that single might lead the listener to the written lyrics after repeated listens, and from those lyrics then to this essay. Finding striking a particular concept I trivially indulged here, that individual might have an idea stoked within to then follow in their own path of investigation and erudition.

This is, of course the best case scenario, and in torturing myself writing a faux dissertation no one requested, I just might have wasted time otherwise spent manufacturing more outwardly accessible content more suitable to cultivating a rap career. Simone White rightfully asks us "to think about the work we have asked the Music [sic] to do, whether it is still able to do that work, and how that work might be done elsewhere" (White 137).[10] I propose this, my music, as a means to avenues elsewhere, not a measuring stick or absolute. Besides, even in essay form this is hip-hop, a practice extending past the music, and we eschew permission as we proceed to give you what you need.

## ix.

*One final moment as I ready the performative tenor of my manifesto voice:*

This is an attempt to pioneer when the idea of no idea being original is unoriginal. This is to propose that originality is to be found in a newfound combination, that we are more than the sum of our reaction videos, more than the deepest fossilized imprint in a sediment of digital replications, used as fuel for top-soil institutional and corporate power. The platform is not the content, and we are not our data. The revolution will not be pitched for a placement on Spotify. It will have to be an arresting experience aware of how to trap attention with multimedia sensory overload. It will appropriate superficiality and put a palatable face to self-inquiring dissociativeness. Refashioning immediacy, it will misdirect to the unconventionally transformative, through a sort of remanning of sound, image, and meaning akin to subliminal messaging. Though of course, any calculus to determine the cocktail of relevancy is elusive in a time like ours, when the right PR budget and/or well-timed controversy can make anything show up at the top of a timeline/media feed.

*Language Arts Unit*, this rap text/book, is a staid stab into this half-opened digital inquiry; staid by the realities of D.I.Y. budgetary concerns, and by an acute awareness of the problems that more complex art presents in communicating a directness. Not every rap album aspires to be catalogued in the Library of Congress, flails itself at genius grants, or vies for consideration as literature. However, this project does. It posits itself and rap as race as form and content, and beyond that a form of theory *and* praxis. It is a personalized linguistic boycott and politics of disengagement, so as to be a challenge to the infatuation with simplification in immediacy, which the ambient, experiential, and potentially arresting nature of the musical form can aptly encounter. While knowing the current streaming paradigm of the musical medium is corporately incentivized (as were past eras), this multimedia effort carries on the longstanding rap tradition of shit-talking by extending that custom to this extrajudicial literary assemblage.

Concretely, a simple and proprietary interactive e-book will accompany the audio correlated to these written words. This will not only fulfill the coexistence and interdependence of these musical raps and their written lyrics as texts, but also evade the hemming of the multimedia nature of the work by conventional music distribution, which though senile and corporate, is masked as a modern and supposedly free-to-play circulatory system. Acknowledging this project's limits impinged by lack resources and renown, this is an elementary example to open the future fold to greater and more collectivized opportunities of refashioning the code from our source, so that we are no longer unwittingly encrypted as dispossessed and passive.

Whether it will be articulated in the from of club banger, discursive essay, hidden camera show, binge-worthy series of episodic video, well-timed meme, fractal selfie collection, or interactive e-book rap album, there is a tangential timeline where— if not already— literacy will cease to mean the capacity to parse solely the written word. When image, sound, and worded fragments hold hands as equal syntactical clauses well past a simple formation of meme— where digital literacy is literacy. That awkward moment when this sentence exists. When you are reading a discursive prose poem and you just can't. Me, an intellectual: categorically horrified and intrigued.

# THE RAPS

# 01:
# Poet-Swordsmith of Baldwin Hills-Crenshaw Mall

*"after about an hour of this frightfully difficult literary labor, he fell to the floor exhausted. we saw him creep, feebly, into the nest of the poems which are always there. so that all this work had not been in vain, we made an examination"*

**it's the poet-swordsmith [of] Baldwin Hills-Crenshaw Mall,
hits but with the shammgod,
dangles phrasing like car alarms**

**it's the poet-swordsmith [of] Baldwin Hills-Crenshaw Mall,
spoken soloist,
three filled notebooks all ajar**

**it's the poet-swordsmith[of] Baldwin Hills-Crenshaw Mall,
hits but with the shammgod,
dangles phrasing like car alarms**

**it's the poet-swordsmith [of] Baldwin Hills-Crenshaw Mall,
spoken soloist,
three filled notebooks all ajar**

I became a brown man in Los Angeles
on a magazine cover,
man-of-color-mumbled through an interview
then fumbled,

my line of scrimmage
down and out counting inches,
became a Black man downtown
with a u-turn
in the business district

between my verse
and spurned romantic interests
whereas certain phone numbers
now have become prison jumpsuit digits,

I'm on a cell reverse translating
my tweets in techno-yiddish,
while I lament solipsism
as a well-educated happy idiot

you never met a wordsmith more illiterate,
reclaimant of ride share privileges,
unemployment benefits,
and breadline manuscripts,
who makes a mean sautéed spinach,

that plate of wine-reduced predilections,
that visage akin
revisionist stone-faced grimace
(like what?)

of the strong silent typography,
apocryphal Olmec and circumspect
to get hemmed denim wet
spit the rawest paroxysms
to focus groupers in headphones

I'm in the gutter club
slanging clichés
the same way a dictionary
rents out ad space
to price human emotion
and contemporary art,

in the gallery as an attendant and
as a pedant I'm a synonym
to [sic] an off-camera Petrarchan rant,
like like like like fuck it, we'll do it live

rewrite the verse from first stanza,
top to bottom,
right to left,
just to just to just to just to just to
get a rise

**it's the poet-swordsmith [of] Baldwin Hills-Crenshaw Mall,**
**hits but with the shammgod,**
**dangles phrasing like car alarms**

**it's the poet-swordsmith [of] Baldwin Hills-Crenshaw Mall,**
**spoken soloist,**
**three filled notebooks all ajar**

# 02:
# The Governor's
# Water Glasses

*shouts out to U.S.V.I. (what up)*

full staffed,
knee taken was
drought tolerant

flag spread,
pole poking my bio-politick

left my theory at that pipeline,
school was prison discourse

niacin in vitamin
my breakfast choice

each morning woke up
spread eagle, yeah, beleaguered
each morning woke up
spread eagle, yeah, beleaguered

**[CHORUS]**
**I spread eagle**
**for the governor's water glasses**
**(spread eagle, yeah, beleaguered)** *[x3]*

**I spread eagle**
**for the governor's water glasses**
**(water, water, water, water, water, water, water)**

spread eagle, yeah, beleaguered,
each morning woke up,
check for FEMA

flood's ~~lines~~ on the foyer,
X on the principal, door
directed deposit,
material benefit liminal

for four score and ye olde yore
posted no bills,
meddlesome weeks' deals,
futures on meals
on wheels

local produce, a metaphor for irony still,
'cause we were shipped in
to front the bill

**[CHORUS]**

I said my brother was a rolling stone,
I was a Standing Rock,
everyday pops came home
and popped that Rolling Rock

he Marshall Planned his Glock,
cleaned it with his TV dinner,
only Black cop to join the blocking line
that electoral winter

facing down the First Nation, all seconds,
safeties ready to empty the chambers,
aquifers languid and tepid

shrugs at state-sanctioned danger:
tears protest gas,
ICE, yeah, money anger

(spread eagle, yeah, beleaguered)

shouts out to that young god Chaac
that made them clouds pop,
condensed our percentage into droplets
to fall on our flock,
cut out the beating heart and
laid it in the pyramid top

yeah, do that to lawmakers
so we can reap crops,
harvest redlined agribusiness,
on subsidized blocks, hot

swiping cards for a single use plastic,
acronyms fail to mention
yo, this water ain't elastic

**[CHORUS]**

I was lead to the content of these pipes
(spread eagle, yeah, beleaguered)

I was lead to the content of these pipes
(spread eagle)

I was lead to the content of these pipes
(spread eagle, yeah, beleaguered)

I was lead to the content of these pipes
(spread eagle, yeah, beleaguered)

I was lead to the content of these pipes
environment, our own terror site

I was lead to the content of these pipes
(spread eagle, yeah, beleaguered)

I was lead to the content of these pipes,
became a victim to my own rights
by their own right

# 03:
# Eyes Dyed in
# Saturated Retinas

**eyes dyed in saturated retinas**
**eyes dyed in saturated**
**eyes dyed in saturated retinas**
**eyes dyed in saturated**
**eyes dyed in saturated retinas**
**eyes dyed in saturated**
**eyes dyed in saturated retinas**
**eyes dyed in saturated**
**eyes dyed in saturated retinas**
**eyes dyed in saturated**
**eyes dyed in saturated retinas**
**eyes dyed in saturated**


eyes dyed in saturated retinas,
blue light of instruments
came from Texas,
it's said that great change to
spawn from the elections,
but sitting on electric fences
don't feel much like a welcome—

head, shoulders, knees, toes
head, shoulders, knees, toes
head, shoulders, knees, toes
my brother's colonists with a candid photo

wading in the water of the
soup of the metrics,
skin tone as an as-needed

hat trick,
family from the old and the new
world ghettos, oppression olympics
medaled in
mementos

my man Solar said we the splash on the canvas,
pilgrim in the freight car bellowing "so it goes,"
up on the pedestal with a brushstroke,
so I guess I'm the kosher Black gesso then—

(eyes dyed in saturated retinas
eyes dyed in saturated)

still to rise,
staid in waiting for the moment
that I blow,
etched a selfie on the front
of the claymore,
combust a musty gesture
of drawings of past pentimentos

I don't see
how I should pay for
this wall that hinders me,
respectfully gone deep in their
non-binary pussy,
I was a drawbridge before
now nondisclosure to agree

still to rise,
staid in waiting for the moment to
hold all the smoke,
alone in two-way mirrors

to share and self-promote,
thinking in an outside voice,
a skinny hunk of flesh of
outside jokes

I don't see
this prescription of ethics over
this lamb over rice,
rationalizing never done saying
the same thing twice,
piecing a detritus self back
for Jamal Khashogghi

I am not the Michael Jordan
of Delaware,

(eyes dyed in saturated retinas)

might be a partial jurist,

(eyes dyed in saturated retinas)

I am unenthused to be looking
laissez-faire in that vanity mirror,

(eyes dyed in saturated retinas)

when it comes to
miscegenating between art forms
(eyes dyed)
I'm a purist

*[featured verse]*

**eyes dyed in saturated retinas**
**eyes dyed in saturated**
**eyes dyed in saturated retinas**
**eyes dyed in saturated**
**eyes dyed in saturated retinas**
**eyes dyed in saturated**
**eyes dyed in saturated retinas**
**eyes dyed in saturated**

---

light-skinned n[]gg[] on the dark web,
GoPro on the pole arm,
megapixel minuscule,
refracting the side arm

in portrait mode
punch a crypto-fascist
in the throat,
esophageal armistice in silo,
bleach blonde endangered rhino

memes on the radio,
gruel in my cup,
double styrofoam half-life
of a video star
binged, upchucked

this that art rock with a
ransom note
through a corner office window

I want all the fire, and the brimstone,
and the fucking smoke

# 04:
# Megabytes Per
# Second Cousin

*"you soon will be a goddamn man,*
*now start learning what life is about now son"*

**[CHORUS]**
**"get smacked 'cause you're blue Black,**
**throwback to welts and twist naps,**
**'n[]gg[],' you**
**ain't allowed to say that,**
**light-skinned with choice**
**to format,**

**"dark-skinned**
**but, yeah, momma passed,**
**crossed the Ward,**
**swept faberge glass**

**"born in that white hospital**
**but they transferred her and I**
**in the moment when crowned**
**my Black ass"**

called my grandfather
for connections,
megabytes per second cousin

I
dialed tone
when I breathed in

and felt my own baggage rushing

I
hung up and slumped over that chair,
staring at that gradient
between forearm and the thigh meat,
the pale yellow dimmed radiance

as if
time was the only gulf between us,
continuity and through-line sequence
medley, bevy of poly-genes
silk-printed just to rerun

mitochondria, yeah, fitted and colloquial,
some preshrunk embodiment,
and all the credentials for a tailor
fitting qualified postmodernists

**[CHORUS]**

Write my own way out of a
brown paper bag
club, race as form
and content,

across a continent
blood ties fists gripped
in blackened love

I
remember those sunny afternoons out
basking just to darken my skin,
comment section effigies of my peers

scrolling minds in tandem

metrics, lines,
self-spurred another scientist with
google image case study basis:
inherent blackness, intrinsic research,
a doubt of predetermined 31 flavors
(sample size per serving,
just a feast of the eyes,
intersections of what swatches
seem to serve and surmise)

with some stubbornness as intuition
or attrition
attributed to affinity
for new scriptures
sketched in books
and doodled verse reliefs,
Black-marked whiteness

prescription lobbying minds
to some greater prophetic margins

two parallel lines
for an abstract
starting

**[CHORUS]**

"soft curls on my neck flap
caress she'd tell me and scratch,
'yeah, boy you look like me
but only back there where them good genes at,'

"brother and sister took after,
we shared features
but the pigment masked us"

**[CHORUS]**

crawfish étouffée in my census identification
written on the back of an SUV double-parked,
a New Orleans gas station

knee-length grass roots
with storm swept down
to the foundation,
charitable body's
[family] records
given to the gulf as a donation

"word,"
of mouth, I remarked
as the portraits I'd yet to see
they met a watery fate,
sweeping the bayou sweat from my
sun-yellowed perplexing pate
I'd yet to contemplate

where does this history start
(no, really)?

and if memory by its very nature
is its own form of art.

# 05:
# Big Rhys

I've saved these memories on blocks:

to come of age in the
Arathi Highlands
with my Guilty Sparks,
ethernet-linked systems
to controller hands

he taught me inverted,
yeah, my Plum dog

was the main cohort
in that digital-to-analog
K-8 bookended by
volumes of all the EB Games trade-ins

and when we snaked through Sotheby's
just toe the line,
and I hugged your mom
the last time

those days of Nightfire and Azeroth—

**so go, video my soul,**
**'cause this was so real, so real**

**and no rush to record,**
**'cause I'm just trying to feel**

**and I can't deal**

match made for an oddball,
holding on until the time expires

to load up an old file
is an old flame
that sparks harmonics on
a heartstring,
you'll see it's worthwhile

suggestion of a trial
to find perchance a reduction
of basic elements through
a concourse of past times

rendered worlds
drawing through-lines
and stuttered sights,
I stand, firmly anti-aliased to rewind

these games have brought
clear resolutions and bleary tears

graphical engines upgrading
as I doubled in years,

and it's strange,
they've given me so much language,
strange how all these moving parts
saved for my own arrangement

still I feel myself anchored,
crazy as it sounds,
I feel myself anchored

12 years-old, docked in Seyda Neen,
my vocal chords now to express
this straining:

the first time I saved face on a cartridge
5 years-old there was moaning in a burning library,
strafing on a Blockbuster-rented
Leon Kennedy on CRT
with barely read ESRB
Big Rhys
on Lyric Avenue between alimony and Tracy

generations of consoles to console
private confirmation hearings,
Marty O'Donnell soundscapes and
West Gash symphonies

**go, video my soul,**
**'cause this was so real, so real**

**no rush to record,**
**'cause I'm just trying to feel**

**and I can't deal**

now now, the Full Frontal Incumbent
thought nothing of it,
akin to something of an electoral puppet,
same script on the notarized budget:
an author's note to a book of rhymes
made public

to obfuscate that collection of overly-abstracted raps
he takes a momentary lapse,
dips the pen inside an inkwell
dwelling on the right reference to
sentimentalize a whole past well

untaxed turns back with mindful inhalations,
citing source awards
with conflagrations

now rejoicing with congratulations for what
moments of childhood are recorded
and then stored

see well, an imaginary shoulder would hark here here,
to tip a solemn head a little there there,
circumnavigating fetal innocence,
transpositions octaves of a younger life
to somewhere more free and bare
(like what?)

**go, video my soul,**
**'cause this was so real, so real**

**no rush to record,**
**'cause I'm just trying to feel**

**and I can't deal**

**I'm documentarian, baby**
**full definition.**

_____

Flood session,
pizza, picture, essen,
retracing sketches
about another epoch:

after school flexing,
index's the weapon,
information passed to
guild raiders and brethren.

Caravan to Karazhan,
tank buffed by power-words,
interior defended
(unseen, unheard).

Stadium Arcadium bumped through
Wet Sand Gateways,
unfurled through curls, braces,
farmer's tans, race bait.

Jumps out of the gym
into punk bedrock,
niche in
silent cartography, maps drawn,
written plots,
pixel polyglot, ravenous mind, stomach,
stopped decibels for gendered interaction,
noiseless pundit.

Fuck kid—

# 06:
# Thrust of the Memos /
# My Domestic Terrorism

*Moziah:*

*well, you know, the KKK is making great strides. you know, I'm a fellow member myself, fellow chapter grandmaster dragon, 32nd degree, in Mississippi, hell, anyhoo. you know, I was thinking about the KKK, and we're making some great strides. we're now accepting Black members and Mexican members, still no Arabs, but you know we're really trying to keep it going. if niggers wanna go back to Africa, well hell, go back to Africa. we liked Marcus Garvey. we, you know, we were his biggest supporter. you know, KKK, we're doing alright. and on that note I gotta git—*

**[CHORUS]**
**thrust of the memos**
**thrust of the memos**
**thrust of the proceeding**
**thrust of the proceeding**
**thrust of the memos**
**(thrust, thrust, thrust)**
**thrust of the memos**
**thrust of the memos**
**thrust of the proceeding**
**thrust of the proceeding**
**thrust of the memos**
**(thrust, thrust, thrust)**

my domestic terrorism
wears Swedish tennis player
Jesus necklace for intersection

my domestic terrorism
wears Swedish tennis player
Jesus necklace for intersection

my domestic terrorism
wears Swedish tennis player
Jesus necklace for intersection

my domestic terrorism
wears Swedish tennis player
Jesus necklace for intersection

my domestic terrorism
wears an AR-15,
hats to make America made in China
make itself a great maker again

my domestic terrorism
buys said bore arm half-off
last mental check-up station

my domestic terrorism
calls free trade's origins in slavery
post-racial

my domestic terrorism
is syndicated, fiber-optic,
distributed through cable

**[CHORUS]**

caged in mylar
we float checkpoints
just joined at the ankle monitor
passing ports for verifications and photos,
toast ICE dangles still from the registry

the thrust of the memos
is an abstraction
for replete liberty
drunk driving doctrines,

an estranged line breaks
formation,
then divorced history

our domestic terrorism
wears a single band of tarnish,
unpolished family film
birthed sovereignty
and a warm embrace of mythos
it privatizes gains and socializes

televangelist separatist statecraft,
all-inclusive in the ethnostate flash
and hate bath

when in Rome
do as the subaltern do
and kneel fast

**[CHORUS]**

# 07:
# Morning Becomes Apoplectic,
# a Follower's Prayer

clock ticks are irrelevant,
settlement, the present tense
deed is an exegesis
with a felt-tipped rhetoric,
scratch and sniff
these ashy palms
smoking desert kiss

placebo christened with that
flick of the wrist

I've been in sediment of the
epoch's layers deep,
carbon copy of my
like page's physique,
a play count as oblique,
all scriptures written cut out
of my abdomen and sewn back
with Rap Genius caesarian annotation

marginal status
with the noose in the lattice,
unconscionable praxis,
theoretics on my axis spin cycle
raining high heavens on my mattress,
drool-stricken mornings
waking up to crusted mouth fractures.

**forgive me for all these scriptures**
**forgive me for all these scriptures**
**forgive me for all these scriptures**
**all sense spent on well wishing**

**forgive me for all—**
**forgive me for all these scriptures**
**forgive me for all these scriptures**
**all sense spent on well wishing**

**forgive me for all—**
**forgive me for all these scriptures**
**forgive me for all—**

**I know I won't be recognized today**

I'm a plot device,
dim foil headdress
refracting upon the headlights,
curved dialogue when protagonists sleep
I'm still up at night

framed in unbeknownst
but rehearsed speech,
crushed dolomite
reading rights to obsequious pardons of
French exits

when mornings become apoplectic
and slept-on electronica
fills a vacuum
I seek the circumspect,
keep my eyes wet in this
moving traffic fishbowl

my optics are shifted 24 hours
in length to catalogue droll

not an allegory to [sic] better circumstances,
a drip-line gushing,
missing pair of blood lancelets,

but a metaphor to [sic]
elementary probabilities,
second chances spun on Quixotic windmills,

an allusion to a minor key,

but an anaphora to [sic] a trudged speed,
a permit to [sic] that concealed weapon.

I am my own epinephrine.

I'm an inverted apostrophe addressed to
no possession,

a series of quotations attributed to
bold-faced irrelevance.

**forgive me for all these scriptures**
**forgive me for all these scriptures**
**forgive me for all these scriptures**
**all sense spent on well wishing**

**forgive me for all—**
**forgive me for all these scriptures**
**forgive me for all these scriptures**
**all sense spent on well wishing**

**forgive me for all—**
**forgive me for all these scriptures**
**forgive me for all—**

**I know I won't be recognized today**

As I bolt my head up to rise
in this time trial,
I humbly seek significance
quantifiable in numbers,

that one of import may walk through turnstiles
and recirculate my thoughts most worthwhile
for those in action of
insights, audience, and reach.

I ask forgiveness for all these scriptures,
all sense spent on well wishing,
minute hands holding hours,
self-immolating auto-da-fés
in the shower.

In the name of the non-gendered parent,
offspring, and all-encompassing spirit of WiFi,
I do ask and beseech.

# 08:
# Nebbish
# Frederick Douglass

*[CHORUS]*
**poet laureate of my living room**
**poet laureate of my living room**
**poet laureate of my living room**
**poet laureate of my living room**

elephant in the hallway,
poet laureate of my living room,
dripping trunk snot,
down-talking the TMC in Khartoum

the nebbish Frederick Douglass
feeling peckish,
techno-yiddish scribbled with a pencil,
vestibule, a threshold of lectures,
lectern as he raps all the measures

reclaimant on the bidet,
shoeless pedant, yeah in the dining room,
on hands and knees with a genuflect,
trademarks phenotypes with Legal Zoom

raps in fugues, sestinas,
Prussian Blue iambs begrudges
antifa farmers market luncheon,
yeah, hair parted like a truncheon

Huey P, à la carte, à la mode Hebdo
in the drawing room
sketching prophets in the margins,
dry humping scripture, yeah well,
on a full moon

pre-fab in the 9th house,
flipping-flopping in a gender neutral blouse,
abstract verse just to out-joust,
just to out-joust

**[CHORUS]**

peanut butter Sandy Koufax
spitting cold facts
in the cryochamber,
no hitter, eight figures rejoined with words,
syntax spinning like an Escher spitter

eschewing monochrome delusions,
every step and footprint a Black realist movement,
expanding bibliography for the duration
of the Uber

talking shop, chewing lipids,
liquid diet sans pill-form stock nonfiction,
placebo freelance eccentric evidence of
a pre-screened well goal post postgrad diction

with a PR firm over my thumb,
facial recognition, yo, on the upswung,
downsized, upsold
solid-state wheezing like just another iron lung

"partate the bars," says the Creole Voltaire,
23 back-up discs, yeah, in the time-share,
single lyric sheet for each sector and hemisphere
with a reading fee so laissez-faire

sitting mid-vacation deloused,
bouncing .wav files, yeah, surfing on a couch,
poet laureate of my living room,
bed and breakfast, yeah, in a random house
motherfucker

**[CHORUS]**

*"ohh, get up or get out the way! I might be in the studio or something, but I'm
still getting hype!"*

*welcome to Langstónia…*

# 09:
# Incredibly Black
# and Extremely Eccentric
# (in Oregon)

*[a short story by Muckraker Jones]*

**incredibly Black and extremely eccentric!**
**Incredibly Black and extremely eccentric...**
**(but where, but where, but where, but where??)**

incredibly Black and extremely eccentric
in Eugene, Oregon,
post-show brunch talking that Eugene Onegin,
so goes the heir apparent Pushkin,
sunlight, an envelope filter
before he cuts out
with his fortune

then continuing to prattle on,
onus is the next mea culpa college town
where they plant and nurture seedlings, outrage farm,
see even the parking ticket was organically sown

split the $50 difference from them usual citations:
footnotes, toenotes, Afro-centric in no sandals lately,
lathe-cut to disrupt,
Portland in the cut,
snapping photos, soundcheck,
self-loather emeritus

after performance de-centered from the whiteness,
bearable lightness watching Insecure with
the finest genuine women, platonic
couch surfers upstream
in a '99 La Saber swimming

just the pale Black negative
Jason Mantzoukas,
Dutch Bros, 5-North,
roses and tulips,

grandest delusions, yo,
went to Bend, Oregon and
found the sound of silence
in audience movements

in Corvallis she reached for my what?
(no, stop, no)

onto the next few days, yo
up the border verily,
Blacked out bookings
amplified group therapy

**incredibly Black and extremely eccentric!**
**(in Oregon)**
**Incredibly Black and eccentric!**
**Incredibly Black and extremely eccentric...**

# 10:
# I Could Rap Forever

*You know what I'm saying? I feel like I could really do this forever.*
*I don't know. I don't know. You know what I'm saying?*

yo, this that ardent cultural marxist
hopping out the fucking starship
in explicit FCC discourse, yeah,
marching in
electoral offices
to the apartments,
bicoastal elite feeling some type of glorious

yo, this that Earl Sweatshirt type beat
(oh my god),
yo, this that overthinking type sack of meat, well,
talking to ya

been off the Internet as of late, so
maybe a little more truth (real talk),
yeah the hangman hungover in the blanks
writing after the shots and shooters saying

I could rap forever,
but I won't (I won't, I won't)

only until the moment in which
my epitaph got a blue check on it,
and bears a likeness of a rapper archetype
in the form of sonnet saying

**I could rap forever,**
**but will you hear?**
**I could rap forever,**
**but will you hear me?**

while the economy is being automated out,
my negro I'm fucking out;
while everything seems to be going down south,
I'ma stay right here and use my mouth,
case in point like
(check one, two, like ok, yeah, ha!):

yo, this that ardent cultural marxist
hopping out the fucking starship (two times!)

clocked out at the happiest hour that can be afforded
when your microphone bag happens to be your wallet,
when no man is the island
that tax brackets use to funnel dollars

well, this that over-his-head-
archipelago-flow-syntax,
great garbage patch of my personality, yeah,
fully intact,
the extinct elephant in the room authorizes
no authority or apps

that's the wrong kind of twist like
intellectual white people dreadlocks
taking naps

**I could rap forever,**
**but will you hear?**
**I could rap forever,**

**but will you hear me?**
**I could rap forever,**
**but will you hear?**
**I could rap forever,**
**but will you hear me?**

*"and now a bright young comic"*

*[featured verse]*

**I could rap forever,**
**but will you hear?**
**I could rap forever,**
**but will you hear me?**
**I could rap forever,**
**but will you hear?**
**I could rap forever,**
**but will you hear me?**

# 11:
# Ignatius Speech

speak up, yes
speak up
speak up, yes
speak up, speak up

**waking up to tea,**
**take the caffeine,**
**why can't I sit down?**

**(no, no, no, no, no, no, no)**

**waking up to tea**
**take the caffeine,**
**why can't I sit down?**

**(no, no, no, no, no, no, no)**

double booked, bagged, and
10 minutes steeped, I said,
"this mind is mine to keep"

though regaled from the
point of sale to your
effigy, no social receipts

I can't seem to bend my knees
or to fold 90 degrees:
a layman lying on a public dais,
spurt open valves in Ignatius speech

another morning pot of tea
that blend you gave to me,
steamed I drunk it all
like a monarch

blank verse leered with
whitened teeth sovereignty—

a full theatrical release,
promotions

well canonized now,
the unraveling performance of
some unclear love poetry

**waking up to tea,**
**take the caffeine,**
**so can't I sit down**

**(no, no, no, no, no, no, no)**

double booked, bagged, and
10 minutes steeped, I said,
"this mind is mine to keep"

though regaled from the
point of sale

*I think that's cool man. It's little like a little interlude…*

# Acknowledgements

This project began as a simple play on words. Little did I know, that in a matter of years it would balloon into this multidisciplinary dramaturgy. In retrospect, it all may be considered a vanity project in its self-spurred and self-funded process. Seeking to innovate, or the very least do something beyond the bare minimum, seems without fail to bring out the ones who cry "why do this much?" or "don't you know people won't care/aren't intelligent/ don't have enough patience?" I see now that this endeavor is for those who whispered, consoled, and shouted on behalf of the other side of those questions.

A simple thanks is not enough for my four loving parents, Marie-Alise, Rick, Wolfram, Kat, and my unendingly cool brother, Kirk, who always motivate me to supersede my previous bests. Their unconditional love is a super-powered, epigenetic force that has pushed me continuously. Including them, there were many who read this work early, from the very first scraps of the book right until the pre-published final draft. Without the luxury of a press or contracted editor to formally edit the piece, I have to thank Alejandro Banuelos, Jonny Collazo, Chocolate Davis, Lily Moayeri, Joseph Natter, Alexander Rowland, Moises Valencia, and Aaron Veerasuntharam for their early, middle, and late-stage impressions on the writing. As well, I give good graces to Max Bell, who offered his proofreading acumen to the foreword essay just before its publication. I am unceasingly grateful to the radical socialist institution, the Los Angeles Public Library, for providing continual refuge from the noise of the world, and facilitating much early evening research after working full days in customer service. Love to my past roommates Caetano Santos, Ethan Quinn, Will Peil, Cameron Hicks, Jason Chung, and Brandon Weiss for bearing with my mood swings, continual audio engineering racket, and general harebrained-ness. Additionally, without the continual banter with my former co-worker and front-of-the-house philosopher Marisela Norte, I don't know if my words and wit would have remained as sharp in the two years crafting this *unit*.

A huge dollop of appreciation to the real mensch Jeff Weiss, who came across my art over two years ago, and has since been an ardent ally and exponent of all I do. He heard the musical album of *Language Arts Unit* in its earliest phases and offered his ear to help me refine it to the emblematic explosion of styles it is now. Though said album was a self-produced effort, the mastering touch of the incomparable Dave Cooley was an honor to have after ceaselessly mixing this record in poorly ventilated apartment a block from a traffic-laden Columbus Route 10 Freeway (in a room where books and this project's paper references almost blocked my speakers and prevented me from properly hearing it all). In this insistence on self-producing the record, the four instrumental compositions outside my own creation are indebted to the talents of alexanderrrowland, kató, and LXMONGRAB. Further, the featured vocals of Aissa Gueye, Chester Watson, Moziah Clark, and Serengeti, the piano wizardry of Ben Salk, and the recording engineering of Derek Sturman, amazingly solidified this musical debut of sorts. Of course, prayer hands emoji to Sara Shewfelt for coming into the picture last minute and snapping some photos to tie the literary and musical halves together.

Finally, I must impress gratitude onto all who contributed to the INDIEGOGO campaign, which held me accountable for finishing this journey through discipline(s): Shane Bernard, Juliet Brooks, John-Henry Carey, Taran Carr, Jonny Collazo, Arian Dehnow, Jaime de Venecia, Lusine Dovlatyan, Ebony Eleanor, Jouquin Fox, Max Friedlich, Pagan George, Russell Goldman, Aissa Gueye, Jamie Hall, DeMille Halliburton, Elijah Holstein, Mallory Isburg, Rob Kanjo, Christopher Malone, Miles McLeod, Steven Meeks, Sam Mendoza Ferguson, Dan Muro, Joseph Natter, Emerson Obus, Chaim Om, Pierre Plantevin, Katherine Kim Podell, Rick Podell, Scody D Prade, Fred Prudhomme, Danielle Pruit, Sarah Rahman, Gina Recasner, Ron Recasner, Matthew Rich, Reece Robbins, Will Schube, Aaron Senfeld, Jonathan Simpson, Simran Singh, Spencer Smyth, Norman Stiles, Eero Talo, Annie Titan, Damon Turner, Ethan Quinn, Sagar Vasishtha, Aaron Veerasuntharam, Chelseaa Vuong, and Martin Weiner.

From an artist who maybe cares a little too much, I give a final thank you to all who read this humble work. May we all give a little more of a shit than we did yesterday.

# Worked Cited/References

## ii.

1.    Mikanowski, Jacob. "Behemoth, Bully, Thief: How The English Language Is Taking Over the Planet." *The Guardian*, Guardian News and Media, 27 July 2018, https://www.theguardian.com/news/2018/jul/27/english-language-global-dominance. Accessed May 2019.

2.    Lanier, Jaron. *Who Owns The Future?* New York: Simon & Schuster Paperbacks, 2014. ; Ibid p. 165; Ibid p. 54 ; Rainie, Lee, and Janna Anderson. "Experts on the Pros and Cons of Algorithms." *Pew Research Center: Internet, Science & Tech*, Pew Research Center, 17 Mar. 2017, https://www.pewinternet.org/2017/02/08/code-dependent-pros-and-cons-of-the-algorithm-age/. Accessed March- August 2019.

3.    Woolf, Virginia, and Susan Dick, editor. "A Dialogue Atop Mount Pentelicus." The Complete Shorter Fiction of Virginia Woolf, 2nd ed., First Harcourt/ Harcourt Brace Jovanovich, 1989, pp. 63–68. ; Arieh-Lerer, Shon. "Why Does Every Hollywood Fantasy Character Have a British Accent?" Edited by Scott McGhee. Uploaded by Slate. *YouTube*, YouTube, 25 Jan. 2018, https://www.youtube.com/watch?time_continue=1&v=xrjuQwkjTYQ Accessed August 2018.. ; Holmes, Jonathan. "Why Are There so Many Posh British Accents in Star Wars?" *WIRED*, WIRED UK, 29 May 2018, https://www.wired.co.uk/article/solo-a-star-wars-story-posh-british-accents-sci-fi. Accessed August 2018. ; Influencer, Instagram. https://coachella.com/ ; Wilderson, Frank B. "Blacks and Master/Slave Relation." *Afro-Pessimism: An Introduction*, Racked & Dispatched, 2017, p. 27. ; Rian Johnson. *Star Wars: The Last Jedi*. Disney,

2017 ; Griffin, Saharra, and Galen Hendricks. "Missing Paychecks Due to Trump Shutdown Total $2 Billion Every 2 Weeks." *Center for American Progress*, Center for American Progress, 30 Apr. 2019, https://www.americanprogress.org/issues/economy/news/2019/01/07/464773/federal-workers-miss-2-billion-every-missed-paycheck-trumps-shutdown/. Accessed May 2019. ; Savage, Dan. "Godwin Suspends Godwin's Law ." *The Stranger*, The Stranger, 19 June 2018, https://www.thestranger.com/slog/2018/06/19/27874178/godwins-law-suspended-by-godwin. ; Keneally, Meghan. "List of Trump's Accusers and Their Allegations of Sexual Misconduct." *ABC News*, ABC News Network, 25 June 2019, https://abcnews.go.com/Politics/list-trumps-accusers-allegations-sexual-misconduct/story?id=51956410. Accessed July 2019. ; ICE. "Advisory Committee on Family Residential Centers (ACFRC)." *ICE*, Immigration Customs Enforcement, 2018, https://www.ice.gov/acfrc. Accessed August 2018. ; Ferullo, Joe. "Three Names Who Changed the Channel on Late-Night TV: Stewart, Colbert and Trump." *TheHill*, TheHill, 30 May 2019, https://thehill.com/opinion/technology/445916-three-names-who-changed-the-channel-on-late-night-tv-stewart-colbert-and. Accessed July 2019. ; Union of Concerned Scientists. "The Climate Deception Dossiers (2015)." *Union of Concerned Scientists*, Union of Concerned Scientists, 9 July 2015, https://www.ucsusa.org/global-warming/fight-misinformation/climate-deception-dossiers-fossil-fuel-industry-memos#.WfickGhSyCo. Accessed July 2019. ; Webb, Kevin. "Amazon's Drone Delivery Service Is One Step Closer to Taking Flight." Business Insider, Business Insider, 5 June 2019, https://www.businessinsider.com/amazon-prime-air-drones-approved-by-faa-2019-6. Accessed May 2019.

4.     Zuckerman, Ethan. "The Internet's Original Sin." *The Atlantic*, Atlantic Media Company, 4 Aug. 2014, https://www.theatlantic.com/technology/archive/2014/08/advertising-is-the-internets-original-sin/376041/. Accessed August 2019. ; Lanier, Jaron. *Who Owns The Future?* Simon & Schuster Paperbacks, 2014, p. 14. ; Hill, Kashmir. "I Cut the 'Big Five' Tech Giants From My Life. It Was Hell." *Gizmodo*, Gizmodo, 7 Feb. 2019, https://gizmodo.com/i-cut-the-big-five-tech-giants-from-my-life-it-was-hel-1831304194. Accessed April 2019.

5.     Lewis, Seth C., and Oscar Westlund. "Big Data and Journalism." *Digital Journalism*, vol. 3, no. 3, 2014, pp. 463, 459., doi: 10.1080/21670811.2014.976418. Accessed 3 June 2019. ; Rainie, Lee, and Janna Anderson. "Experts on the Pros and Cons of Algorithms." *Pew Research Center: Internet, Science & Tech*, Pew Research Center, 17 Mar. 2017, https://www.pewinternet.org/2017/02/08/code-dependent-pros-and-cons-of-the-algorithm-age/. Accessed March- August 2019. ; Hamblin, James. "It's Everywhere, the Clickbait." *The Atlantic*, Atlantic Media Company, 11 Nov. 2014, https://www.theatlantic.com/entertainment/archive/2014/11/clickbait-what-is/382545/. Accessed July 2019.

## iii.

1.     Nielsen Holdings. "Nielsen Music Mid-Year Report U.S. 2019." June 2019. ; Young, Kevin. "Blacker Than Thou." *Bunk: the Rise of Hoaxes, Humbug, Plagiarists, Phonies, Post-Facts, and Fake News*. Graywolf Press, 2017, p. 389.

2.   Jenkins, Craig. "Migos' Culture II Isn't an Album, It's a Data Dump."
     *Vulture*, Vulture, 30 Jan. 2018, https://www.vulture.com/2018/01/migos-
     culture-ii-isnt-an-album-its-a-data-dump.html. Accessed October 2018.


3.   Masters, Marc. "In Retrospect We Should've Called Small Label Music
     "music" and Major Label Music "dependent Music."" *Twitter*. December
     30, 2018. https://twitter.com/Marcissist/status/1079426593662001153.
     Accessed December 30, 2018 ; Debord, Guy. "Spectacular History". *The
     Society of the Spectacle*. Translated by Ken Knabb. Zone Books, 2002, p.
     50.


4.   Felix, Doreen St. "Black Teens Are Breaking The Internet And Seeing
     None Of The Profits." *The FADER,* The FADER, 25 Oct. 2017, https://
     www.thefader.com/2015/12/03/on-fleek-peaches-monroee-meechie-
     viral-vines. Accessed May 2019. ; Monroe, Peaches. "Eyebrows on Fleek
     Vine by Peaches Monroee." Uploaded by Sweater Gahd. *YouTube*,
     YouTube, 29 July 2014, https://www.youtube.com/watch?
     v=dfBdBpr7KCo. Accessed May 2019. ; Jefferson, Margo. "Ripping Off
     Black Music." *Harper's Magazine*, Harper's Magazine, Jan. 1973, https://
     harpers.org/archive/1973/01/ripping-off-black-music/. ; "Transgender
     Women of Color at Stonewall." *Equality Archive*, Equality Archive, 12 Oct.
     2017, https://equalityarchive.com/history/transgender-women-of-color-
     at-stonewall/. Accessed June 2019.


**iv.**

1.   Zisook, Brian. "Underground Hip-Hop Is Dead-Welcome to the
     Mainstream." *DJBooth*, 27 Nov. 2017, https://djbooth.net/features/
     2017-11-27-underground-hip-hop-is-dead. Accessed August 2018. ; Levy,
     Lauren. "The Gatekeepers of SoundCloud Rap." *Vulture*, Vulture, 6 Dec.

2018, https://www.vulture.com/2018/12/the-gatekeepers-of-soundcloud-rap.html. Accessed May 2019. ; Rys, Dan. "How Warner Bros., Tha Lights Global & a Gang of Influencers Catapulted Lil Pump to Stardom." *Billboard*, Billboard, 1 Dec. 2017, https://www.billboard.com/articles/business/8054683/lil-pump-tha-lights-global-warner-bros-influencers. Accessed May 2019. ; Knopper, Steve. "A Hip-Hop Signing Frenzy Sends New Record Deal Prices Soaring." *Billboard*, Billboard, 29 Mar. 2018, https://www.billboard.com/articles/business/8272682/hip-hop-signing-frenzy-record-deal-prices-soaring. Accessed May 2019. ; Snowden, Scott. "Greenland's Massive Ice Melt Wasn't Supposed To Happen Until 2070." *Forbes*, Forbes Magazine, 16 Aug. 2019, https://www.forbes.com/sites/scottsnowden/2019/08/16/greenlands-massive-ice-melt-wasnt-supposed-to-happen-until-2070/#5ce1df454894. Accessed August 2019. ; Dana, Felipe. "Tracking the Melt in Greenland's Ice Sheet – in Pictures." *The Guardian*, Guardian News and Media, 21 Aug. 2019, https://www.theguardian.com/environment/gallery/2019/aug/21/tracking-the-melt-in-greenlands-ice-sheet-in-pictures. Accessed August 2019. ; Anderson, Trevor, and Gary Trust. "Winner's Circle: Lil Nas X's 'Old Town Road' Breaks Record With 17th Week Atop Billboard Hot 100." *Billboard*, Billboard, 29 July 2019, https://www.billboard.com/articles/columns/chart-beat/8524235/lil-nas-x-old-town-road-longest-number-one-hot-100. Accessed August 2019 ; O'Connor, Roisin "Post Malone Breaks Streaming Records with New Album Beerbongs and Bentleys." *The Independent*, Independent Digital News and Media, 7 May 2018, https://www.independent.co.uk/arts-entertainment/music/news/post-malone-beerbongs-and-bentleys-album-stream-number-one-record-breaking-drake-more-life-a8339721.html. Accessed March 2019. ; Beaumont-Thomas, Ben. "Drake Beats the Beatles' 1964 Record for Most US Top 10 Hits in a Year." *The Guardian*, Guardian News and Media, 23

Oct. 2018, https://www.theguardian.com/music/2018/oct/23/drake-beats-the-beatles-1964-record-for-most-us-top-10-hits-in-a-year. Accessed March 2019.

2.     Debord, Guy. "Time and History", "Spectacular Time". *The Society of the Spectacle*. Translated by Ken Knabb. Zone Books, 2002, p. 41-52. ; Fukuyama, Francis. *The End of History and The Last Man*. Perennial, 1992. ; Ra, Sun. "Sun Ra - Space Is the Place (1974)." Uploaded by Thelonseometraveller, *YouTube*, YouTube, 4 Mar. 2019, https://www.youtube.com/watch?v=bCalqwsicls. Accessed July 2019. ; T, Pusha. "Pusha T – The Story of Adidon." *Genius*, Genius , 29 May 2018, https://genius.com/Pusha-t-the-story-of-adidon-lyrics. Accessed August 2018. ; Pusha, T. "Pusha T - The Story of Adidon [Drake Diss]." Uploaded by Music Tapez, *YouTube*, YouTube, 17 Oct. 2018, https://www.youtube.com/watch?v=w4XH3LYIeDA. Accessed May 2019. ; Tenpas, Kathryn Dunn. "Tracking Turnover in the Trump Administration." *Brookings*, Brookings, 7 Aug. 2019, https://www.brookings.edu/research/tracking-turnover-in-the-trump-administration/. Accessed August 2019. ; Law, Tara. "These Presidents Won Electoral College But Not Popular Vote." *Time*, Time, 15 May 2019, https://time.com/5579161/presidents-elected-electoral-college/. ; Cain, Áine. "Trump and Kanye West Have Something in Common That Sets Them Apart from Most Other Highly Successful People." *Business Insider*, Business Insider, 2 May 2018, https://www.businessinsider.com/donald-trump-kanye-west-reading-books-2018-5. Accessed October 2018.

3.     Bandini. "Rappers Might Start Going To Jail Because Of Their Lyrics." *Ambrosia For Heads*, Ambrosia for Heads, 16 Apr. 2019, https://ambrosiaforheads.com/2019/04/rapper-convicted-for-lyrics/. Accessed

July 2019. ; Strauss, Matthew. "Tay-K Sentenced to 55 Years in Prison for Murder." *Pitchfork,* Pitchfork, 23 July 2019, https://pitchfork.com/news/ tay-k-sentenced-to-55-years-in-prison-for-murder/. Accessed July 2019. ; Weiss, Jeff. "Stabbing, Lies, and a Twisted Detective: Inside the Murder Trial of Drakeo the Ruler." *The FADER*, The FADER, 17 July 2019, https:// www.thefader.com/2019/07/11/drakeo-the-ruler-murder-trial-los- angeles-report. Accessed July 2019.


**V.**

1.      Black Star. "Twice Inna Lifetime" *Mos Def & Talib Kweli Are Black Star.* Rawkus, 1998.


2.      Gaillot, Ann-Derrick. "There's Sprite at The Cookout." *The Outline,* The Outline, 16 Apr. 2018, https://theoutline.com/post/4174/sprite-black- advertising-history. Accessed June 2019. ; Ink, Shy. "Meet Bhad Bhabie's Main Collaborator Brittany B." *Genius,* Genius, 16 Sept. 2018, https:// genius.com/a/meet-bhad-bhabies-main-collaborator-brittany-b. Accessed May 2019 ; Cole, J. "J. Cole x Lil Pump Interview at The Sheltuh." Uploaded by J. Cole, *YouTube,* YouTube, 25 May 2018, https:// www.youtube.com/watch?v=RNIQU-7y9Fo. ; Espinoza, Joshua. "Ebro Calls 6ix9ine a 'Spectacle' and 'Car Accident,' Threatens to Expose Who 'Finances' Him." *Complex*, Complex, 10 Oct. 2018, https:// www.complex.com/music/2018/09/ebro-calls-6ix9ine-spectacle-car- accident-expose-who-finances-him. Accessed May 2019. ; Weiser, Benjamin, and Ali Watkins. "Tekashi 6ix9ine Pleads Guilty and Agrees to Cooperate With Prosecutors." *The New York Times*, The New York Times, 1 Feb. 2019, https://www.nytimes.com/2019/02/01/nyregion/tekashi-69- pleads-guilty.html. Accessed May 2019.

3.    Moten, Fred. "The Case of Blackness." *Criticism*, vol. 50, no. 2, 2009, p. 177., doi:10.1353/crt.0.0062. Accessed July- August 2019.

4.    Laver, Mark. "Lil Nas X and the Continued Segregation of Country Music." *The Washington* Post, WP Company, 20 June 2019, https:// www.washingtonpost.com/outlook/2019/06/20/lil-nas-x-continued-segregation-country-music/. Accessed July 2019 ; Grabar, Henry. "But, What Do the Black Working-Class Voters of Youngstown, Ohio, Think?" *Slate Magazine*, Slate, 16 June 2019, https://slate.com/news-and-politics/ 2019/06/black-voters-youngstown-ohio-trump-democrats.html. Accessed July 2019 ; Mooney, Paul, and Dave Chapelle. "Chappelle Show Everybody Wanna Be a Nigga Funny Clips By Mellow." Uploaded by MELLOW DBG, *YouTube*, YouTube, 23 Nov. 2016, https:// www.youtube.com/watch?v=7cv90tFOUlY. Accessed July 2019.

5.    Wang, Amy X. "America Isn't Ready for Asian Rappers. They're Taking Over Anyway." *Rolling Stone*, Rolling Stone, 19 Aug. 2019, https:// www.rollingstone.com/music/music-features/88rising-joji-kris-wu-asian-rap-takeover-727420/. Accessed March 2019. ; Hanauer, Larry, and Lyle J. Morris. "China in Africa." *RAND Corporation*, RAND Corporation, 12 Mar. 2014, https://www.rand.org/pubs/research_briefs/RB9760.html. Accessed May- June 2019. ; Chandran, Nyshka. "China Says It Will Increase Its Military Presence in Africa." *CNBC*, CNBC, 27 June 2018, https:// www.cnbc.com/2018/06/27/china-increases-defence-ties-with-africa.html. Accessed May 2019 ; Handy, Gemma. "Antigua: Sprawling 'Chinese Colony' Plan across Marine Reserve Ignites Opposition." *The Guardian*, Guardian News and Media, 20 June 2019, https:// www.theguardian.com/world/2019/jun/20/antigua-yida-project-chinese-colony-controversy. Accessed July 2019. ; Spencer, Richard. "Gavin's a

Straight Shooter, Fam. Https://T.co/4FfLtHfepD." *Twitter*, Twitter, 11 Mar. 2017, https://twitter.com/richardbspencer/status/840688627281715201? lang=en. Accessed February 2019. ; Mansell, Henry. "Eminem Becomes RIAA's Second-Highest Selling Singles Artist Of All Time." *HipHopDX*, HipHopDX, 1 Mar. 2018, https://hiphopdx.com/news/id.46095/ title.eminem-becomes-riaas-second-highest-selling-singles-artist-of-all-time. Accessed May 2019.

6. Sesali, B. "Flirting With Blackness." *Feministing*, Feministing, 17 July 2015, http://feministing.com/2015/07/17/flirting-with-blackness/. Accessed May 2019.

7. Bastién, Angelica Jade. "How the Thurgood Marshall Film Misunderstands Colorism." *Vulture*, Vulture, 19 Oct. 2017, https://www.vulture.com/2017/10/marshall-misunderstands-colorism.html. Accessed October 2018. ; Angus, Haaniyah. "The Biracial Aesthetic: Colorism and Hollywood." Edited by Chichi Amaena, *Medium*, Medium, 23 July 2018, https://medium.com/@hanxine/the-biracial-aesthetic-colorism-and-hollywood-ebe00725cd0b. Accessed July 2019.

8. Appiah, Kwame Anthony. "Rooted Cosmopolitanism." *The Ethics of Identity*, 1st ed., Princeton University Press, Princeton, NJ, 2005, p. 256.

9. Chesman, Donna-Claire. "Juice WRLD Wants to Be Known as 'Less of a Rapper' and 'More as a Musician.'" *DJBooth*, DJBooth, 29 Oct. 2018, https://djbooth.net/features/2018-10-29-juice-wrld-more-than-a-rapper. Accessed March 2019. ; Cowen, William. "ASAP Rocky on His Experimental New Album: 'I Don't Just Rap, I Actually Make Music.'"

*Complex*, Complex, 1 June 2018, https://www.complex.com/music/
2017/10/asap-rocky-on-experimental-new-album. Accessed March 2019.

10.   Wilderson, Frank B. "Blacks and Master/Slave Relation." Afro-Pessimism:
      An Introduction, Racked & Dispatched, 2017, p. 30


**vi.**

1.    Beatty, Paul. "Chapter 24". *The Sellout*. Farrar, Straus and Giroux. 2015, p.
      277.


2.    (After writing several drafts, I retroactively sought sources for these
      sentences and thoughts. While I could find revolving doors of
      experiences and theories across black manuscripts, I found these were
      my own approximate unfurlings from deeply personal searches. If that
      claim makes my efforts less scholastic or comprehensive, I welcome the
      risk in purporting some origination.)


3.    Abreu, Manuel Arturo. "Online Imaged Black English." *Arachne,* Arachne,
      September 1, 2015. https://arachne.cc/issues/01/online-
      imagined_manuel-arturo-abreu.html. Accessed August 2018. ; Young,
      Kevin. "The Age of Euphemism." *Bunk: the Rise of Hoaxes, Humbug,
      Plagiarists, Phonies, Post-Facts, and Fake News*. Graywolf Press, 2017, p.
      447, 435, 442.


4.    Williams, (Stacey) Saul. "Coded Language" *Amethyst Rockstar*. American
      Recordings. 2001


5.    Glover, Donald. "Teddy Perkins." *Atlanta*. FX. 2018.

6.     White, Simone. *Dear Angel of Death*. 1st ed. Ugly Duckling Presse, 2018,
       p. 149 ; Moten, Fred. *In the Break: The Aesthetics of the Black Radical
       Tradition*. University of Minnesota Press, 2003. ; Hartman, Saidiya. "The
       Burdened Individuality of Freedom". *Afro-Pessimism: An Introduction*,
       Racked & Dispatched, 2017, p. 35-36.

## vii.

1.     Rushdy, Ashraf, and Benjamin Waite. "The Art of the Public Apology." *The
       Conversation*, The Conversation, 19 Sept. 2018, https://
       theconversation.com/the-art-of-the-public-apology-90425. Accessed July
       2019. ; James, Caryn. "TESTING OF A PRESIDENT: THE SPEECH; Apology
       and Defiance Echo a Nixon Addres." *The New York Times*, The New York
       Times, 18 Aug. 1998, https://www.nytimes.com/1998/08/18/us/testing-
       of-a-president-the-speech-apology-and-defiance-echo-a-nixon-
       address.htm. Accessed July 2019. ; Massey, Wyatt. "Hulk Hogan
       Apologizes for Racist Remarks." *CNN*, Cable News Network, 25 July 2015,
       https://www.cnn.com/2015/07/24/entertainment/hulk-hogan-wwe-
       apology-racism-feat/index.html. Accessed July 2019.

2.     Young, Kevin. "The Age of Euphemism." *Bunk: the Rise of Hoaxes,
       Humbug, Plagiarists, Phonies, Post-Facts, and Fake News*. Graywolf Press,
       2017, p. 447, 435, 442.

3.     Olmstead, Molly. "Georgia Lawmaker Who Shouted Racial Slurs in
       Shocking Who Is America? Segment Will Resign." *Slate Magazine*, Slate,
       25 July 2018, https://slate.com/news-and-politics/2018/07/georgia-rep-
       jason-spencer-to-resign-after-who-is-america-segment.html. Accessed
       March 2019. ; Chapelle, Dave. *"Season 2 Episode 7."* Chapelle's Show.
       Comedy Central. 2004.

4.　Goggin, Benjamin. "From Porn to 'Game of Thrones': How Deepfakes and Realistic-Looking Fake Videos Hit It Big." *Business Insider*, Business Insider, 23 June 2019, https://www.businessinsider.com/deepfakes-explained-the-rise-of-fake-realistic-videos-online-2019-6#in-january-2018-a-deepfake-creation-desktop-application-called-fakeapp-launched-bringing-deepfakes-to-the-masses-a-dedicated-subreddit-for-deepfakes-also-gained-popularity-3. Accessed July 2019. ; Nagesh, Ashitha. "Finland Basic Income Trial Left People 'Happier but Jobless.'" *BBC News*, BBC, 8 Feb. 2019, https://www.bbc.com/news/world-europe-47169549. Accessed May 2019.

5.　Dinkins, Stephanie. "Conversations with Bina48." *STEPHANIE DINKINS*, STEPHANIE DINKINS, 2014, https://www.stephaniedinkins.com/conversations-with-bina48.html. Accessed March, July-August 2019. ; Tiffany, Kaitlyn. "Virtual Influencers Have Got to Be a Fad - Right?" *Vox*, Vox, 3 June 2019, https://www.vox.com/the-goods/2019/6/3/18647626/instagram-virtual-influencers-lil-miquela-ai-startups. Accessed August 2019.

## viii.

1.　Swasy, Alecia. "I Studied How Journalists Used Twitter for Two Years. Here's What I Learned." *Poynter*, Poynter, 25 Mar. 2017, https://www.poynter.org/tech-tools/2017/i-studied-how-journalists-used-twitter-for-two-years-heres-what-i-learned/. Accessed June 2019. ; Yong, Ed. "What Was Lost in Brazil's Devastating Museum Fire." *The Atlantic*, Atlantic Media Company, 5 Sept. 2018, https://www.theatlantic.com/science/archive/2018/09/brazil-rio-de-janeiro-museum-fire/569299/. ;

Boissoneault, Lorraine. "A Brief History of Book Burning, From the Printing Press to Internet Archives." *Smithsonian.com,* Smithsonian Institution, 31 Aug. 2017, https://www.smithsonianmag.com/history/brief-history-book-burning-printing-press-internet-archives-180964697/. Accessed August 2019 ; The Reporters Committee for Freedom of the Press. "Governments Continue to Come up with New Ways to Prevent Access to Records." *The Reporters Committee for Freedom of the Press*, The Reporters Committee for Freedom of the Press, 2 Apr. 2013, https://www.rcfp.org/journals/governments-continue-come-n/. Accessed July 2019 ; Emery, David. "George W. Bush White House 'Lost' 22 Million E-Mails?" *Snopes.com*, Snopes, 11 Oct. 2016, https://www.snopes.com/fact-check/g-w-bush-lost-22-million-e-mails/. Accessed July 2019 ; Lanier, Jaron. "Siren Servers." *Who Owns The Future?* New York: Simon & Schuster Paperbacks, 2014, p. 53-57 ; Neal, Mark Anthony. "'If You Don't Own the [Servers]": Curating Aggregating Doing Black Studies in the Digital Era ." *NewBlackMan (in Exile)*, NewBlackMan (in Exile), Apr. 2014, https://www.newblackmaninexile.net/2017/04/if-you-dont-own-servers-curating.html. Accessed June 2019; Folkenflik, David. "News Media Wrestle With How To Describe Some Of Trump's Tweets." *NPR*, NPR, 16 July 2019, https://www.npr.org/2019/07/16/742109324/news-media-wrestle-with-how-to-describe-some-of-trumps-tweets. Accessed July 2019. ; Wolffe, Richard. "Out of Control? Or Is Trump's Tweeting Designed to Distract?" *The Guardian*, Guardian News and Media, 4 Mar. 2017, https://www.theguardian.com/us-news/2017/mar/04/donald-trump-tweeting-designed-to-distract-russia-obama. Accessed October 2018. ; Hat, Ass. https://twitter.com/realDonaldTrump. Accessed?

2.     "Research Grants & Sponsored Programs at the MSU Library." *MSU Library*, Montana State University, 2018 https://www.lib.montana.edu/

about/library-research/. Accessed June 2019 ; Clark, Jason. "'RE:Search

Unpacking the Algorithms That Shape Our UX." *RE:Search Unpacking the*

*Algorithms That Shape Our UX,* Institute of Museum and Library Services,

Montana State University, 2017, https://www.imls.gov/sites/default/files/

grants/re-72-17-0103-17/proposals/re-72-17-0103-17-full-proposal-

documents.pdf. Accessed June 2019 ; "Internet Society 2019 Global

Internet Report" *Internet Society,* Internet Society, 2019, https://

future.internetsociety.org/2019/. Accessed June, July 2019. ; EQUAL Skills

Coalition. "I'd Blush If I Could." *UNESCO,* UNESCO, 25 June 2019, https://

en.unesco.org/Id-blush-if-I-could. Accessed July 2019. ; Lanier, Jaron.

*Who Owns The Future?* New York: Simon & Schuster Paperbacks, 2014, p.

9 ; Ibid. p. 192. ; Snow, Jackie. "'We're in a Diversity Crisis': Cofounder of

Black in AI on What's Poisoning Algorithms in Our Lives." *MIT Technology*

*Review,* MIT Technology Review. February 14, 2018. https://

www.technologyreview.com/s/610192/were-in-a-diversity-crisis-black-in-

ais-founder-on-whats-poisoning-the-algorithms-in-our/. Accessed

October 2018.


3.      Isaac, Mike, and David Yaffe-bellany. "The Rise of the Virtual Restaurant."

*The New York Times,* The New York Times, 14 Aug. 2019, https://

www.nytimes.com/2019/08/14/technology/uber-eats-ghost-

kitchens.html. Accessed August 2019. ; Union of Concerned Scientists.

"Where Are Self-Driving Cars Taking Us? (2019)." *Union of Concerned*

*Scientists,* Union of Concerned Scientists, 2019. https://www.ucsusa.org/

clean-vehicles/self-driving-cars/AV-equity. Accessed August 2019. ;

Porter, Jon. "Amazon Patents 'Surveillance as a Service' Tech for Its

Delivery Drones." *The Verge,* The Verge, 21 June 2019, https://

www.theverge.com/2019/6/21/18700451/amason-delivery-drone-surveillance-home-security-system-patent-application. Accessed August 2019.

4.    Alexander, Michelle. *The New Jim Crow: Mass Incarceration in the Age of Colorblindness.* 2nd ed. New York, NY: New Press, 2012.

5.    Peck, Morgen. "Cryptocurrency Is Not Just a Boys' Club." *Glamour*, Glamour, 14 Mar. 2019, https://www.glamour.com/story/meet-the-women-of-cryptocurrency. Accessed July 2019 ; Stafford-Langan, Rosalie. "Crypto Goes Mainstream: What Big Finance Is Doing." *Financial News*, Financial News, 9 Aug. 2018, https://www.fnlondon.com/articles/what-the-biggest-financial-institutions-are-doing-about-cryptocurrencies-20180807. Accessed July 2019. ; Coleman, Lauren deLisa. "Inside The Shadowy World Of Race, Hate And Cryptocurrency." *Forbes*, Forbes Magazine, 22 Mar. 2018, https://www.forbes.com/sites/laurencoleman/2018/03/22/inside-the-shadowy-world-of-race-hate-and-cryptocurrency/#215201d4545c. Accessed July 2019.

6.    Hao, Karen. "China Has Started a Grand Experiment in AI Education. It Could Reshape How the World Learns." *MIT Technology Review*, MIT Technology Review, 3 Aug. 2019, https://www.technologyreview.com/s/614057/china-squirrel-has-started-a-grand-experiment-in-ai-education-it-could-reshape-how-the/?utm_source=pocket-newtab. Accessed August 2019. ; Schroeder, Ray. "Emerging Roles of AI in Education." *Inside Higher Ed*, Inside Higher Ed, 19 June 2019, https://www.insidehighered.com/digital-learning/blogs/online-trending-now/emerging-roles-ai-education. Accessed August 2019. ; Lanier, Jaron. "From Below." *Who Owns The Future?* New York: Simon & Schuster Paperbacks, 2014, p. 94-97 ; Zirin, Dave. "LeBron's Education Promise Needs to Become This Country's

Promise." *The Nation*, The Nation, 2 Aug. 2018, https://
www.thenation.com/article/lebrons-education-promise-needs-become-
countrys-promise/. Accessed August 2019.

7.     Cannizzaro, Sara. "Internet Memes as Internet Signs: A Semiotic View of
       Digital Culture." *Significant Systems Studies*, vol. 44, no. 4, 2016, pp. 562–
       586., doi:10.12697/sss.2016.44.4.05.; Knobel, Michele, and Lankshear,
       Colin. "Memes and Affinities: Cultural Replication and Literacy
       Education.", 2006 pp. 1–23., https://www.researchgate.net/profile/
       Colin_Lankshear/publication/
       249902174_Memes_and_affinities_Cultural_replication_and_literacy_ed
       ucation/links/00b495343791f6ab3e000000/Memes-and-affinities-
       Cultural-replication-and-literacy-education.pdf. ; Freire, Paulo. "Chapter
       3." *Pedagogy of the Oppressed*, Continuum, 2005, p. 104.

8.     Khan, Rumi. "The Alt-Right as Counterculture: Memes, Video Games and
       Violence." *Harvard Political Review* , Harvard Political Review , 6 July 2019,
       https://harvardpolitics.com/culture/alt-right-counterculture/. Accessed
       July 2019. ; Wong, Julia Carrie. "8chan: The Far-Right Website Linked to
       the Rise in Hate Crimes." *The Guardian,* Guardian News and Media, 5
       Aug. 2019, https://www.theguardian.com/technology/2019/aug/04/
       mass-shootings-el-paso-texas-dayton-ohio-8chan-far-right-website.
       Accessed August 2019. ; Salazar, Adan. "Soros Views 'Nation-State as
       Problem,' Wants 'One World Government' Solution: US State Senator."
       *Alex Jones' InfoWars*, InfoWars, 24 Nov. 2017, https://www.infowars.com/
       soros-views-nation-state-as-problem-wants-one-world-government-
       solution-us-state-senator/. Accessed August 2019 ; Shapiro, Ben. "What a
       One-World Government Looks Like." *Townhall*, Townhall.com, 26 Oct.
       2011, https://townhall.com/columnists/benshapiro/2011/10/26/what-a-

one-world-government-looks-like-n1329916. August 2019 ; Beck, Glenn. "One-World Government in Our Future?" *Glenn Beck*, Glenn Beck, 7 May 2018, https://www.glennbeck.com/content/articles/article/198/33297/. Accessed August 2019 ; Wallace, George. "Inaugural Address of Governor George Wallace, Which Was Delivered at the Capitol in Montgomery, Alabama." *Alabama Textual Materials Collection*, Alabama Textual Materials Collection, 2010, http://digital.archives.alabama.gov/cdm/singleitem/collection/voices/id/2952/rec/5. Accessed March, August 2019.

9.    Kennedy, Gerrick D. "Appreciation: Nipsey Hussle's Dreams Were Bigger than Hip-Hop." *Los Angeles Times*, Los Angeles Times, 1 Apr. 2019, https://www.latimes.com/entertainment/music/la-et-ms-nipsey-hussle-appreciation-20190401-story.html. Accessed July 2019. ; Arango, Tim. "Nipsey Hussle Was Hailed as a Peacemaker by the LAPD. He Was Also Their Focus in an Investigation." *The New York Times*, The New York Times, 15 July 2019, https://www.nytimes.com/2019/07/15/us/nipsey-hussle-investigation.html. Accessed July 2019.

10.   White, Simone. *Dear Angel of Death*. 1st ed. Ugly Duckling Presse, 2018, p. 137.

# Sources Consulted, Cracked, or Considered

Cooper, Brittney C., Susana M. Morris, and Robin M. Boylorn. *The Crunk Feminist Collection*. New York City: Feminist Press at the City University of New York, 2017.

Davis, Chocolate. *Repudiations and Exultations*. Vol. 1. Langstónia: The Estate.

hooks, bell. *Feminist Theory: From Margin to Center*. South End Press, 1984.

A melange of NPR, a Few Cold Brew Lattes, A Liberal Arts Degree

Morgan, Joan. *When Chickenheads Come Home to Roost: a Hip-Hop Feminist Breaks It Down*. 1st ed. Simon & Schuster 1999.

Ra, Sun. *This Planet Is Doomed*. New York: Kicks Books, 2011.

Rose, Tricia. *The Hip Hop Wars: What We Talk About When We Talk About Hip Hop*. 1st ed. BasicCivitas, 2008.

Said, Edward. *Representations of the Intellectual*. Vintage Books. 1994

Somebody, Everybody. twitter(dot)com. Somewhere, Everywhere: Now- The End

Žižek, Slavoj. *Violence*. Picador, 2007.

# Images

(photo by Sara Shewfelt)

**Rhys Langston Podell** is a multidisciplinary artist and performer born, raised, and based in Los Angeles, California. Publications such as The LA Times, AFROPUNK, LA Weekly, and LA Record Magazine have praised his musical efforts. As a visual artist, his work has been passed over by the best in the business. A graduate of Wesleyan University in Middletown, Connecticut, he remains the poet laureate of his living room and has a higher vertical leap than your favorite rapper. Hitherto unpublished, he is unwavering and oft unintelligible.